LAC
BV
4211.2
.F57
1979
Asian

P9-DHJ-021

Wallace E. Fisher

Who Dares to Preach?

The Challenge of Biblical Preaching

DISCARDED

No Longer

APU

Property

AUGSBURG Publishing House • Minneapolis

PROPERTY OF AZUSA PACIFIC UNIVERSITY
AZUSA, CALIFORNIA

MARSHBURN MEMORIAL LIBRARY
AZUSA PACIFIC UNIVERSITY
AZUSA, CALIFORNIA 91702

WHO DARES TO PREACH?

Copyright © 1979 Augsburg Publishing House

Library of Congress Catalog Card No. 79-54112

International Standard Book No. 0-8066-1769-1

All rights reserved. No part of this book may be used or reproduced in any manner whatsoever without written permission except in the case of brief quotations embodied in critical articles and reviews. For information address Augsburg Publishing House, 426 South Fifth Street, Minneapolis, Minnesota 55415.

Scripture quotations unless otherwise noted are from the Revised Standard Version of the Bible, copyright 1946, 1952, and 1971 by the Division of Christian Education of the National Council of Churches.

NEB refers to *The New English Bible* © the Delegates of the Oxford University Press and the Syndics of the Cambridge University Press, 1961, 1970.

GNB refers to the *Good News Bible: The Bible in Today's English Version* © American Bible Society 1966, 1971, 1976.

MANUFACTURED IN THE UNITED STATES OF AMERICA

To my hard-pressed colleagues in the ministry, 1945-1985, whom I respect firmly, and to our replacements, 1970-2010, whom I envy a bit because their good fight promises to be stiffer than ours. Perhaps they will learn more quickly than we did to value the "weapons of our warfare" (2 Cor. 10:3-6 KJV),

and

To our Reforming Fathers—Luther, Calvin, Knox, and Zwingli—who recovered in their time and place the primacy of preaching and teaching from the Early Church, and to Melanchthon who fashioned in 1530 at Augsburg one of the most enduring confessions of the Faith in Christendom,

and

To the congregation of the Lutheran Church of the Holy Trinity in Lancaster, Pennsylvania, whose active Christian witness in America dates from 1730, whose seventeenth senior pastor I am privileged to be in their 250th anniversary year, and whose gallant response to biblical preaching called this book from countless dialogues into this more permanent form.

Contents

Foreword by Gabriel Fackre 7

Preface 10

Introduction 14

PART ONE
PREPARING THE PREACHER

1—Preaching, the World, and the Church 24

2—Preaching in Today's Theological Context 39

3—The Preacher's Call and Office 57

4—The Preacher's—and the Congregation's—
Need to Grow 73

5—On Preparing to Prepare the Sermon—Part I 83

6—On Preparing to Prepare the Sermon—Part II ... 98

PART TWO
PREPARING AND PREACHING THE SERMON

7—The Biblical Sermon: What Is It? 114

8—The Sermon: Its Structure 130

9—The Sermon: Its Introduction,
Conclusion, and Title 143

10—The Word of God and the Preacher's Words 160

Now, Finally 178

Notes 182

Bibliography 194

Foreword

THE CURRENT REVIVAL OF PREACHING is long overdue. The spiritual hungers of culture and congregation would have been met, and the taste for cotton candy mysticisms and pietisms avoided, if we had been about this fundamental task of the pastor. Wallace Fisher has been trying to tell us this for twenty years in his writing and lecturing on mission and renewal. Perhaps we shall listen to him now when he devotes himself to this first love of his own ministry in what may be his most important book.

The thing that makes this such a compelling work is the context out of which it rises. I know something about that setting, having been a comrade in mission with the author and the remarkable congregation he serves. Together we marched for human rights, debated Carl McIntyre, organized a citizens' newspaper, shared the lecture platform, the pulpit, and labored along the evangelism frontier. The wisdom in this book is hard-won, tested in the social and theological laboratories of the twentieth century. It comes out of a matrix in which both pastor and people have exercised that rare gift of being *both* faithful and fruitful, unafraid to speak and do the Word in the face of the world's hostilities and apathies, yet able to change lives, circumstances, and institutions. There is no cheap talk between these covers; these words have made a profound difference in one place, and can, and will, now have that impact on the larger church.

At the center of all Wallace Fisher has to say about preaching is the Word. The Word, most fundamentally, is Jesus Christ, the eternal Logos made flesh. The Word in its larger meaning is the Good News of the deeds of God from creation to consummation which environ the Incarnate and atoning Act, what the author calls, the "God-story." And the Book of that Story is where he calls us to hear the Word. Thus "biblical preaching" is the controlling vision for what is said here, "fidelity to God's Word."

But this is no biblicism trading on the anti-intellectualism and authoritarianism of the hour. Fisher rejects the literalist abuse of the Bible and urges the preacher to make honest use of the best critical tools of scholarship. Further, since the God of the Bible is the Lord over and in history, the author calls the preacher to engagement with history as the context for fidelity. For one, robust preaching requires the reading of history. But more, we are to keep God company in history, immersed in the personal and public encounters which illuminate what we read in the Book about God's definitive acts from Exodus to Easter. As in Fisher's own ministry, the pastoral and prophetic undergird the preaching office.

In our struggle today to recover the biblical and theological, it is tempting to give honor to the "substantive" and disdain the methodological. This is short-sighted indeed, for the theologian needs the practitioner and vice versa. It is particularly refreshing to find them in Chalcedonian union. They are so joined in this work. The theological explorations and the biblical imperatives of the office of preacher are linked to important discussions of the craft of sermon-making: preparation, choosing the right words, beginning and ending. Again, holism makes its presence felt.

"Who dares to preach?" Yes, you will get searching answers to that question in this book. But the reader will find more than that. There is a rich vein of ore to be mined here for those who are digging into a deeper question: How can one be a faithful minister of the Gospel in the late twentieth century?

> GABRIEL FACKRE,
> Professor of Theology
> Andover Newton Theological School
> Newton Centre, Massachusetts

Preface

I HAVE BECOME MORE AWARE of my debt to others with each book I have written. Where I could recall those debts specifically, I have done so in the body of the book, the footnotes, and the bibliography. But the human mind absorbs more than we realize. Like a magnet, it attracts and holds ideas that we adopt unconsciously as our own. I thank those unremembered persons as eagerly as I have thanked the others by name, especially the members of the congregation I serve.

My secretary, Ms. Arline S. Fellenbaum, deserves large thanks for taking this manuscript through several drafts as does Ms. Patricia S. Baker, our office secretary, who helped generously. These clergy colleagues with whom I now serve or have served in Trinity Church recalled some aspects of our discussions on preaching which would otherwise have been lost to the presentation and sharpened the clarity of the manuscript: Larry L. Lehman, B. Penrose Hoover, and Milton R. Wilkes, presently on Trin-

ity's staff; and R. Ray Evelan, Jack R. Hoffman, Hugo W.
Schroeder, Jr., former colleagues. Other clergy friends
have also improved the manuscript: Charles F. Drawdy,
Guy S. Edmiston, Jr., Gabriel Fackre, James N. Gettemy,
Donald R. Heiges, Richard E. Koenig, F. Dean Leuking,
Duke McCall, Howard J. McCarney, James I. McCord,
Lawrence R. Recla, Berwyn H. Russell, Jr., Theodore F.
Schneider, Priscilla Shoup, Harald S. Sigmar, William R.
Snyder, Joanne P. Stenman, William H. Stotler, John H.
Tietjen, D. Elton Trueblood, and Edward F. Weiskotten.
These lay persons helped, too: David L. Balch, Robert L.
Baughan, Jr., Robert and Sally Desch, Craig and Mary
Lou Dyer, Melvin J. Evans, Paul Mark Fisher, John H.
Garofola, M.D., Ruth Grigg Horting, the Honorable Paul
A. Mueller, Jr., Elvin and Ann Musselman, William and
Phyllis Whitesell, Jack and Dorothy Williams, and Robert
H. Witmer, M.D.

A preface is more than a traditional appendage if it
places the author and his work in their historical-existential setting.

My basic qualifications for writing this book on preaching are like those of other parish pastors. But I do have
two vocational qualifications that are not characteristic
of most clergy in my generation. First, I have served in
the same center-city church for twenty-eight years—the
Lutheran Church of the Holy Trinity, Lancaster, Pennsylvania, a metropolitan community of 350,000 persons. This
250-year old congregation—confronted, challenged, and
sustained by biblical preaching and evangelical teaching
—discovered new life in the Word in the early 1950s, and
has, over two succeeding decades, gone forward steadily
in enlarging its ministry to persons in Christ's Name.[1] The
laity as well as the clergy in Trinity Church testify that
the prow of the congregational ship during these decades

of deepening renewal and widening community service has been biblical preaching. Written in and from this context the book is seasoned by the grandeur and misery of front-line ministry.

Second, my continuing dialog with pastors in several hundred clergy conferences in the United States, Canada, and Europe over the last quarter century also informs and shapes this book. The ordering of the material—shared, discussed, corrected, and augmented over four separate years in the middle 1960s and early 1970s when I served as guest professor of homiletics for graduate students at the Lancaster Theological Seminary (United Church of Christ) and the Gettysburg Theological Seminary (Lutheran Church in America)—places me under obligation to my students in those formal teaching situations. Earlier drafts of chapters 1 through 4 have also been shared, discussed, and improved in clergy conferences at Princeton Theological Seminary, the Southern Baptist Seminary at Louisville, the Yokefellow House in Richmond, Indiana, the Perkins School of Theology in Dallas, the Lutheran School of Theology at Chicago, and in scores of regional clergy conferences throughout the United States.

Now, a word about sexist language. Jesus reveals a God who creates, through faith in his Son, a community of equals, not men lording it over women but brothers and sisters serving one another and others for Christ's sake.[2] Galatians 3:28 and Acts 2:17-18 are basic biblical texts. Reformation theology is also a leveler. Priesthood is not an order but a function; all Christians, male and female, are ministers of Christ. Occasionally, I have used the word man generically in this book. Where it does not blunt the force of the language or appear to be awkward, I have used words like lay person, people of God, part-time ministers, full-time ministers, and so on. I have also used the double pronoun, male and female, deliberately at many points for teaching purposes. Since language reveals what we feel as well as what we think about God, persons, and the world, we shall have to work to do those concrete tasks in church and society that demonstrate God's attitude toward persons, male and female, white, black, red, and yellow, elderly and young, imprisoned, enslaved, and politically free. From this basic renewal will come a new language that speaks readily of all persons as equals in God's sight, each having an intrinsic dignity.

Finally, I acknowledge gladly my debt to my wife, Margaret Elizabeth Stauffer Fisher. Sharing with me two and three times a week in worship hours in Trinity parish and in some interdenominational assemblies around the nation, she has heard me preach more than three thousand times! She has done so with unfailing grace, good humor, and critical support. Margaret—a disciplined student of the Scriptures and faithful in daily prayer, an avid reader in literature and biography, a recognized leader in church and community affairs, and a sought-after public speaker—has been from the beginning of my ministry a creative critic. She is God's best human gift to me and our son, a strong contributor to Trinity Church, the community of Lancaster, and those who are encouraged by this book.

WALLACE E. FISHER
Lancaster, Pennsylvania

Introduction

Finally, I decided that the point of all this, the point of theology, the point of the institutional church, the point of the parish or congregation is to bring the good news to the world so that the world will have the One worth worshiping to worship.
        —John Snow

NATURE AND PURPOSE OF THE BOOK

THIS BOOK IS ABOUT BIBLICAL PREACHING; the heralding of the good news

- that God was in Jesus of Nazareth reconciling the world to himself;
- that in Christ God's Word is spoken fully in history;
- that in Christ liberation is offered to the people of all races;
- that in Christ human lives are changed as radically today as in biblical times;
- that in Christ our sins are forgiven, our new creaturehood is given, the sting of death is removed;
- that Christ is Lord of the scriptures, the church, and the world;
- that God's Spirit works mediately through his Word; and

• that God's kingdom, a corner of it now present in Christ's church, will come in its full power and glory when he chooses.

Biblical preaching is not the declaration of theological propositions to which the hearers are expected to give intellectual assent, or the use of Bible texts as pretexts, or the cursory survey of a passage of Scripture passed off as expository preaching. Biblical preaching, essentially the God-story, is also the church's story about God through the ages and the preacher's story about his or her experience of God.

Biblical preaching is Trinitarian. Much contemporary preaching is not. It focuses on the Redeemer, nods occasionally to the Creator, and is oblivious to the person and work of the Holy Spirit.[1] This "preaching," especially in mainline Protestantism, ignores the Old Testament and the apocalyptic book of Revelation. It focuses on the gospels and epistles. Biblical preaching, on the other hand, takes the whole Bible as the Spirit-prompted human record of God's self-revelation in history. The biblical preacher reads and interprets the full biblical record in the light of Jesus' life, teaching, death, and resurrection. But the sermon that begins in the Bible and stays in the Bible is not biblical.[2] The sermon that begins in the world (life-situation) and never gets into the Bible is not biblical either. Nor is preaching grace without law or law apart from gospel biblical.

Biblical preaching shows how God acted in the past so that we can discern his deeds in our moment of history and learn how we might expect him to act in the future. While it focuses on persons-in-society, it does not offer a blueprint for personal behavior, social action, or worship. Nor does it provide a timetable for Christ's second coming. The biblical sermon brings us into a personal relationship with the God who creates, redeems, and guides us to be his people and, as individuals in community, to fashion a just society for the sake of his kingdom. It empowers us to act morally without being moralistic. The biblical "sermon (like art) effects a new kind of seeing. The ethical imperative, to be sure, is present, but as corollary to recognition. . . . There is in the Christian Gospel the closest correspondence between receiving and giving." [3] Biblical preaching—setting forth the whole counsel of God (demand and promise)—is historically rooted, theologically serious, culturally aware, celebrative, always existential. "When God's Spirit breathes on men and women they testify to God's promises and demands which he has made known fully in Christ." [4] Biblical preaching is effective. This does not mean that the preacher's objectives are always realized! But it does mean that God's Word never returns void.

God acts anew in our moment of history through biblical preaching, evangelical teaching, and the sacraments. His Spirit, acting through his Word, employs these earthly means.[5] But if preaching is to be fully biblical, it must also reflect the preacher's conviction and it must certainly be spoken in the idiom of the people, using concrete images from the hearers' daily experience. In biblical preaching, Christ himself appeals through a particular preacher to people in a particular congregation to decide, in their freedom, for or against him. Biblical preaching is an ongoing activity of God in our time and situation.

What has been said here should not be taken as an attempt to *define* biblical preaching. We have only provided clues to its nature, content, and purpose. I shall attempt to *describe* biblical preaching more fully throughout the book. Christ appealing through flesh and blood people defies definition which, by its nature, imposes precise boundaries and limits. The workings of the Spirit are defined only by God.

This book reflects the hard-won knowledge that learning to preach biblically is a life-long affair. No one is born to it. There are different gifts among us and some men and women are more disciplined in the faith than others, but all preachers have had to learn—and go on learning to the end of their earthly ministry—the what, why, and how of biblical preaching. Because of the wealth of insightful biblical studies, unprecedented technological changes, and shock-inducing social changes during the last forty years, biblical preachers will have gained deeper perceptions of God, man, and culture. Their preaching style will have altered over the years to keep the shape of the message, the cultural images, and the language relevant to the people they preach to. The Word of God is unchanging; the *proclamation* of the Word is ever changing.[6]

This book then is about *our* learning to preach biblically. It addresses the day by day ministry of men and women whose talents are adequate but not brilliant, whose persons are steady but not scintillating, whose egos reach out to Christ yet veer away on self-serving errands often enough to convince us and our parishioners that we are not holy messengers of God but human messengers of the holy God. The book testifies that one need not be a James Stewart, a William Coffin, a Gardner Taylor, or a Frederick Buechner to proclaim the whole counsel of God effectively.

THE STRUCTURE OF THE BOOK

In our discussion of biblical preaching we shall focus on the deceptively simple question, "Who Dares to

Preach?" Examining five basic elements in biblical preaching in the American parish, we shall probe the person of
the preacher as public self, social self, family self, and private self and inquire how these facets of personhood
come together or collide as he or she responds to God's
call first to be a Christian person and then to be a Christian minister in our society. We shall ask by whose authority anyone presumes to preach. We shall also inquire how
the preacher discerns the divine Word in the Spirit-
prompted human words of the Bible, proclaims it boldly,
teaches it in depth, and provides pastoral care from its
resources in a culture radically different from that of the
early church. We shall examine how the biblical preacher
employs human words of his or her own choice as vehicles
for God's Word to individuals-in-community at a time
when the English language is debased. Throughout this
study, we shall identify the spiritual self-disciplines and
assess the grueling intellectual and emotional labor required to do biblical preaching. I have made little effort
to systematize these elements; they are inexplicably bound
together in parish ministry. They also intertwine because
I have chosen to write a reflective book on biblical
preaching.

There are margins of mystery around biblical preaching and evangelical teaching. We shall probe them; we
cannot dispel them.

Though this book is written with the preacher in mind,
lay members can also find help in it. Discovering how demanding it is for anyone to preach God's Word responsibly year after year in our culture, they will ask intelli-
gent questions and offer helpful suggestions that will
hearten their pastor, and their intercessory prayers will
strengthen him or her in preparing and preaching sermons. They will also become more perceptive hearers and

enlightened doers of the Word. The book can encourage and equip lay people to proclaim God's promises and demands in their homes, shops, business offices, factories, laboratories—wherever people gather.

Christian preaching is not fully effective until it is done corporately to individuals and institutions in the world. Prophetic ministry is not antithetical to pastoral ministry; the dichotomy of social gospel and personal gospel is not biblical. Every chapter attempts to make this clear. A silent church in a political society which, contrary to its constitution and political ideals, is frequently guilty of violating human rights at home and abroad, exploiting the middle-class, catering to the wealthy, and keeping its poor dependent is neither a responsible corporate citizen nor a true Christian community. At the same time, a church that does not care for its own members from the resources of God's Word and engage in person-to-person evangelism is not the healing-teaching fellowship of Christ.

THE AUTHOR'S STANCE

Falling into the hands of the gracious God is not like a holiday in the highlands of Scotland or a vacation in Aspen, Colorado. It is more like falling in love, getting married, and raising a family—exhilarating, demanding, nurturing, frustrating, fulfilling. God's grace is free; it is not cheap. Telling God's truth in love to people who are conditioned to cliches, sophistry, manipulation, and falsehood; describing Christ's values to people who are culturally conditioned to a material way of looking at life; and addressing God's Word to social-political issues in white, middle, and upper class congregations (Protestant, Roman Catholic, Orthodox)—while ministering to them and living with them as friends and depending on them for one's means of support—is the hardest work I know.

What I have written in this book is a summary of what I have learned over the years. My journey as a *preacher* has not been smooth. A detour into full-time college teaching in a secular field years ago was, I recognized later, an effort to escape the *preaching* ministry. Returning to the parish ministry by way of "College Church" in the community where I had served as a faculty member, the preaching ministry remained, for me, a heavy burden for years. I did it painstakingly, but I did it grudgingly. Preparing sermons and preaching them was an obedient deed. Some fifteen years ago, for reasons I do not fully understand, preaching became a joy as well as a burden. It remains a heavy responsibility to be sure, but it has become also a distinct privilege. Both strands in my experience run through these reflections on biblical preaching.

But struggles of this sort—stemming from a variety of causes—are not sufficient reasons for preachers to throw in the sponge. It has always been demanding on one's *self* to preach God's Word to others, in any political society, at any time. Our best efforts, like those of other preachers before us, turn out often enough to be plodding, sweaty, partial failures. There is anguish in our preaching. But there is joy and confidence, too, for in our well-intentioned, hard-fought partial successes, God's Spirit enables us to testify to Christ in our moment of history—and human lives are changed. Because God's Spirit is present in biblical preaching, such preaching catches a reflection of Christ in Gethsemane, picks up the rustle of his garments as he strides from the tomb, sounds a note or two in the symphony of his smashing victory over sin and death. So, it pleases God in this generation, as in all generations before us, to liberate and empower willing persons to serve humanity through "the foolishness of preaching."

At the same time, we are under obligation to God, his people, and ourselves to see that our preaching "is not more foolish than it need be. . . . A sermon . . . which has not our uttermost best in it, which is not written and prepared with a responsible sense of its part in the saving purpose of the Most High, is not preaching, but merely the routine fulfillment of a professional task." [7] Even so, our best efforts fall short.

> ⟨ Nothing that is worth doing can be achieved in our lifetime; therefore we must be saved by hope. Nothing which is true or beautiful or good makes complete sense in any immediate context of history; therefore we must be saved by faith. Nothing we do, however virtuous, can be accomplished alone; therefore we are saved by love. No virtuous act is quite as virtuous from the standpoint of a friend or foe as it is from our standpoint. Therefore we must be saved by the final form of love which is forgiveness. [8] ⟩

The revival of the church in the West waits for a powerful, widespread revival of biblical preaching in the Protestant, Roman Catholic, and Orthodox churches in the closing decades of the twentieth century. And it may be—given the grim realities of nuclear armed states, dwindling material resources, and the population explosion—that human life itself will be decided in these decades by the world's response to biblical preaching. [9]

PART ONE

Preparing
the
Preacher

1 Preaching, the World, and the Church

The lamps are going out all over Europe; and we shall not see them lit again in our life-time.
—Sir Edward Grey, on the eve of World War 1

It is Lambeth's duty to remind Westminster that Westminster is responsible to God.
—William Temple

Christendom had done away with Christianity without being aware of it.
—Søren Kierkegaard

MINISTERS WHO WANT TO BE BIBLICAL PREACHERS in the closing years of the twentieth century confront complex problems unique to this age. In the four decades since Bonhoeffer asked how one can preach in a "secular way" about God to "man come of age," Western society has become more secular: more scientific, sensate, technological, revolutionary, fragmented. Theoretical and technological science has advanced more in the last forty years than in the preceding five thousand years of recorded history.[1] The social, economic, political, and religious climate reflects the incalculable shock of that reality. In this era values and relationships have changed more quickly than they could be defined. Robert J. Lifton calls modern man, "Protean

24

man," because, like the Greek god Proteus, he alters his shape to suit any situation, refusing to adapt to any one form, thereby losing contact with his real self.[2]

Part of the contemporary preacher's problem is to preach biblically in this unstable culture that is radically different from the culture in which the first generation of Christian preachers proclaimed the now "old, old story of Jesus and his love." The story *is* old in an era when people are conditioned to think that new is best and old is useless. Built-in obsolescence and voracious consumerism are part of our economy. Our cultural mind-set is locked to the here and now: get and do what you want; live with gusto; play now, pay later. What is real to contemporary Americans is what they hear, touch, taste, see, and smell. Peter Berger put it this way: "Whatever the situation may have been in the past, today the supernatural as a meaningful reality is absent or remote from the horizons of everyday life of large numbers, very probably of the majority of people in modern societies. . . ."[3]

The writers of the New Testament, no less than the writers of the Old Covenant, had a wholly different outlook from ours. Their view of the world and history was *eschatological* ("My kingdom is not of this world," to be distinguished from the "other-worldly" view dominant in Medieval faith) as well as *temporal* ("The kingdom of God is among you"). Even so, the mind-set that the early church faced was not hospitable to God's good news. The first-century heralds of God stirred intellectual criticism of their message among the "rational" Greeks, the first people to call the gospel "foolishness." The Greeks disdained a God who, subject to Rome's authority, could be betrayed, denied, forsaken, scorned, spit upon, and crucified by mortals. The gospel, a stumbling block to the

Pharisees, was pure nonsense to the Greeks. It was not good news; it was "foolishness."

The Christian message is also a stumbling block and folly to millions today who have no time for the God who came into history (Incarnation) making it the revelation of his person (Resurrection). Too many church people, preachers among them, equate moralizing with biblical preaching. Mainline Protestant preachers have ignored the eschatological dimensions of the New Testament thereby impoverishing the church, while preachers of the literalist persuasion have misrepresented the gospel of Jesus by using the books of Daniel and Revelation as timetables for the end of the world.[4]

Millions of people, including the churched, do not appear to be interested in discerning God's purposes, accepting his promises, obeying his commands, or looking to the full coming of Christ's kingdom.

How can the critical-minded preacher hope to get a positive response from hearers who, like the preacher, are culturally conditioned to a world of sense and time? How can he or she find adequate language to communicate the God event so that it interests, attracts, and persuades musicians and merchants, bus drivers and lawyers, suburban mothers with little children and aggressive prostitutes on Times Square, twenty-year-old feminists who admire Gloria Steinem and grandmothers who adore Lawrence Welk, hard-drinking advertising executives with ulcers and bored assembly-line workers with high blood pressure? Jesus and his world are unreal to "Protean man," secular people, people "come of age," and technological people. That is a substantial barrier preachers face today, often in themselves. They must level or get across it to preach effectively. They must get the Jesus-story out of the first century into the twentieth century.[5] And they must do this without compromising its essential and historical character, while communicating its existential meaning. We are able to discern and meet the Resurrection Christ in the theology of John and Paul because of the "historical" Jesus we find in the gospels.

To complicate further the contemporary biblical preacher's task, most of his or her hearers lack any strong sense of history. Jacques Barzun observes bluntly that "the historical sense in modern populations is feeble or nonexistent . . . even though the mania for keeping records, building archives, and celebrating trivial anniversaries is rampant."[6] People today, some clergy as well as others, tend to devalue or disdain tradition—both Christian and national—pursuing privatism above community.[7] This problem is especially difficult to cope with in communicating the gospel because Christianity is a historical faith. A nation whose people disdain history and a church that forgets God's mighty deeds in yesteryear lose their collective identities as amnesia victims lose their personal identities. Consequently, they are neither interested in nor able to face the future. Christopher Lasch observes that our current disposition to devalue the past is "one of the most important symptoms of (our) cultural crisis. Drawing on historical experiences, he demonstrates that "a denial of the past proves on closer analysis to embody the despair of a society that cannot face the future."[8]

Those ministers who breach this cultural barrier must shrug off their weariness only to wade through centuries of conflicting church traditions and stacks of current biblical studies to get at the story itself.[9] Many of these biblical studies will structure and enflesh, inform and correct one's preaching, but parish preachers must find the *time* to assimilate the insights they provide (Chapters 5 and 6). Then, each preacher must find the human words *and* put them together in order to persuade people that the Jesus "story"—shaped originally to a three-tiered universe in which demons possessed human beings, angels delivered supernatural messages, and God became man—is relevant in a world with three-and-a-half billion people, a third of whom are locked into subhuman existence because, in part, "Christian" nations exploited their lands and peoples in the past and are now indifferent toward them, and all of whom live on a small planet in an unimaginably vast cosmos that physicists tell us is running down. That in itself is an awesome task.

But the biblical preacher's work is made still more difficult because he or she knows that our world is closer to George Orwell's predictions in *1984* (written in 1949) and those of Huxley in his *Brave New World* (written in 1948) than most people realize. Genetic and behavioral engineering portend a stable social order without personal freedom, security without creativity, sex without love and/or passion, art without form, literature without meaning—in short, existence without life. Harvard's influential behavioral psychologist, B. F. Skinner, declared recently: "We have not yet seen what man can make of man." That is a frightening prospect in the perspective of this century's man-made wars, genocide, mass imprisonments and/or liquidation of political dissidents, atomic destruction of Hiroshima and Nagasaki, nuclear stockpiles, totalitarian states, exploitation of nature, and mass starvation. Caught in this escalating depersonalization, only those ministers bold enough to make the leap of faith can testify that Christ is the way, the truth, and the life, *and,* at the same time, have confidence that the human activity of preaching Christ can be effective. Even these discover quickly that the contemporary gods competing with the Christian God are more sophisticated and powerful than the gods of the Amorites, Babylonians, Greeks, and Romans: the computer, the test tube, behavioral conditioning, genetic engineering, the bomb, the military-industrial complex, the multi-national conglomerates, power, pleasure, drugs (including alcohol and nicotine), and a faceless-mindless bureaucracy in government, education, and the church are strong adversaries. The Huxley-Orwell-Skinner gods (thought control, behavioral control, genetic control) crowd the Father of our Lord, Jesus Christ, from the lives of the people to whom we preach.[10]

Gabriel Vahanian summarizes concisely this human condition of technological people:

> Having left behind the universe of myth for that of technique, contemporary man, bewildered, exposes himself to the constraints of a two-fold change: the change is religious to the extent that Christianity, though once deeply involved in a civilization now moribund, is nonetheless implicated in the rise of the technological phenomenon. The change is cultural to the extent that the technological phenomenon, though bound up with Christianity, nonetheless appears to constitute the ultimate negation of the very civilization through which Christianity reached an apogee of sorts.[11]

Then, too, our era is polluted by words. Why add more to those that already weary us? This question becomes especially pressing when serious preachers who work carefully with words discover how badly words have been debased since World War I. Why pour out twelve to fifteen hundred-million more ambiguous words every Sunday from 500,000 Protestant, Roman Catholic, and Orthodox pulpits when so many people, churched as well as unchurched, are culturally conditioned to distrust not only what politicians, educators, labor leaders, industrialists, and newscasters say, but also what their friends, doctors, employers, preachers, and mates say? Preachers must wrestle with this complex social-psychological problem or the act of preaching will become an ineffectual routine "professional" task.

Shortly after Harry Truman became president of the United States, he called for "a moral and spiritual awakening in the life of the individual and in the councils of the world," declaring in his brash way that "there is no problem on this earth tough enough to withstand the claim of a genuine revival of religious faith. . . ." If President Truman had stopped there, his plea would have lacked substance. But he got specific. He called for "an Isaiah or a St. Paul to awaken this sick world to its moral and spiritual responsibility." [12]

Mr. Truman, knowingly or not, spoke from a biblical perspective. A genuine renewal of the church and consequent revival of human decency among our citizens depend on biblical preachers, ordained and lay, who are sensitive enough and knowledgeable enough about their post-Christendom world to ache with the tension between it and their treasured values of the Scriptures, and yet have been rendered hopeful enough by their Scriptures to believe that these modern principalities and powers cannot separate persons from the love of God-in-Christ. That hope undergirds their conviction that God's Spirit can use the old, old story in the human activity of preaching to gather new disciples. On that hope the church was planted around the Mediterranean world. On that hope the church has discovered the secret of being born again generation after generation. Unless the drama of salvation is told relevantly and persuasively; unless the story of Jesus and his love is handed on in intelligible forms from this generation to the next; and unless it gets into the daily experience of the people, the awareness of God's creative work and confidence in his redeeming deed in Christ will fade from memory in America in another several generations as it basically has in so many parts of Europe.

Biblical preaching depends on God's searing and healing Word. His Word alone can liberate persons from the tyranny of the Huxley-Orwell-Skinner gods. But God's Word requires preachers who, committed to it themselves, learn how to proclaim it persuasively and teach it intelligibly. People cannot be saved without hearing the law and the gospel; they cannot know God's demands and promises without effective heralds. People cannot decide for or against Christ until they hear his true story and actually see him as he *is*.

There are tens of thousands of homilies "delivered" every Sunday in the United States, but there appears to be precious little biblical preaching. The laity, as well as the clergy, bear heavy responsibility for this indifferent attitude toward biblical preaching. Many do not relish it because it is concrete, specific, confrontational. Like their unchurched neighbors, they want to be soothed with words. "As cats and dogs like to be stroked, so do some human beings like to be verbally stroked at fairly regular intervals." [13] Many in this generation prefer smooth words from their "prophets." They are especially sensitive when the preacher, girded in God's truth, makes judgments about their indulgent life-styles, racism, materialism, and narcissistic religious behavior, or suggests that America is "not the darling of Divine Providence." [14]

American Christianity in the 1950s and the early 1960s was middle-class white togetherness fashioned by a widespread drive for affluence in suburbia. Biblical preaching was in eclipse. Enthusiastic lay devotees of "cultural re-

ligion" put piety on the Potomac and built thousands of
new churches in growing suburbia, letting the center-city
fend for itself. Secular piety thrived, church budgets
soared, numbers evangelism flourished, but there was no
widespread revival of the church in America in the 1960s.
In spite of the work of the World and National Councils
of Churches, local parishes became more parochial, narcissistic, and success-oriented. Racial violence broke out
first in Little Rock (1957), then in Birmingham, Watts,
Newark, Detroit, Chicago, Memphis, and Washington,
D.C. Outrunning the boundaries of race, students revolted
on campus after campus from Berkeley to Cambridge as
America's undeclared war in Vietnam dragged on inter-
minably. But more often than not, the church closed out
the critics and the rebels. In those places where biblical
preaching was done many comfortable members closed
their minds against it and, criticizing those who had the
courage to do it, found congregations more to their liking.

Here and there signs of church renewal appeared, but
renewal was not concentrated in any region of the United
States or in any Protestant denomination. Reform rather
than renewal characterized both Protestant and Roman
Catholic churches. Most "evangelical" churches espoused
personal religion. Many of their lay members allied themselves with the political right. When the Watergate scan-
dal forced President Nixon to resign, Billy Graham, called
on to explain his uncritical friendship with Mr. Nixon,
announced that he was a New Testament evangelist, not
an Old Testament prophet. But Graham's dichotomy was
not confined to "evangelicals." [15] Rooted in a false understanding of God's ongoing self-revelation, it is also characteristic of mainline Protestants and Roman Catholics.
Jesus, the man nobody knew in the 1930s and 1940s, became a buddy—"Are You Running with Me, Jesus?"—in

the 1950s and, in most American communities, a stalwart defender of the status quo in the 1960s. To millions of Americans in the late 1960s—especially former church members, disillusioned youth reared in the church, white liberals, Black revolutionaries and minorities in general, student critics of the Vietnam War, women, and disenchanted clergy—the church was the problem. It remains so for millions of Americans.

This problem has been in the making at least since the middle of the last century.[16] Decade after decade, as the time-honored values of Western society began to crumble, the church retreated, except for forays here and there, to save its institutional life. The "Christian Century," promised by church leaders in 1900 and the "Century of Progress," heralded by the secularists turned out to be a century of horrors: the nightmare of trench warfare and poison gas, worldwide economic depression, concentration camps from Dachau to the Gulag Archipelago, slave labor, genocide, saturation bombings, terrorism, and nuclear blackmail. People everywhere in the West—their perception of the Christian God dead or dying as Nietzsche had predicted—gave their allegiance to false gods, subscribed to inhumane philosophies, were mesmerized by illusion-making psychologies, valued social order above social justice, and a minority turned to the occult or terrorism to get what they wanted.[17] The church, accommodating itself to this world or turning its back on it, offered no viable alternative. These conscious and unconscious flights from personal and social responsibility helped to shatter persons and fragment society. By 1970, David Schon, an American psychologist, could declare that "in the central aspects of our lives our sense of personal constancy is collapsing and our social stability is going to pieces." In view of the present nuclear arms race, diminishing natural resources, and growing disparity between the rich and poor nations, some social critics judge that we are living now in a *pre-war* era.

The big question about the relevance of Christianity and the church and preaching is inextricably bound into the crisis in Western culture which began in the sixteenth century. Neither the Reformation leaders nor the Roman Catholic reformers established an in-depth dialog with Renaissance man in the critical, coming-alive, geographically-expanding sixteenth century. Machiavelli was a practicing Roman Catholic. His treatise, *The Prince*—summarized, "the end justifies the means"—did not prevent the Roman Catholic Church from burying him as one who had "died in the faith." Bacon, Descartes, and Newton—professing Christians to the end of their lives—enlarged this widening cultural breach in the seventeenth century. In the eighteenth century, Voltaire's rationalism, Hume's skepticism, Franklin's deism, and Jefferson's religious rationalism made inroads into American culture, side-by-side with "religious" revivalism. As American culture became more rationalistic and humanistic, the church became more anti-intellectual and dogmatic in some quarters and more humanistic in others.

In the nineteenth century, Friedrich Nietzsche, Karl Marx, Sigmund Freud, and Charles Darwin, and in the twentieth century Albert Einstein—their way already prepared—emerged quickly as the heralds of new and powerful gods in the once Christian West. Nietzsche, pronouncing God dead, called for a revision of all values. Marx, espousing dialectical materialism and attacking Christianity frontally as the "opiate of the people," laid the foundations for a radically different socio-political order purged of private and corporate capitalism and "Christianity." Freud denied every human's transcendental qualities; for him, religion was an illusion that had no future. Darwin presented a new version of "time," dogma, and cosmology. Herbert Spencer, a thorough-going rationalist, promptly applied Darwin's theory of evolution to society. Albert Einstein discovered spatial and temporal relativity (social corollary: all knowledge is conditioned by the viewpoint of the knower). Relativism in social studies was, in part, a consequence of Einstein's theory of relativity in physics. The church failed to come to grips with these direct and indirect criticisms of its medieval concepts, talked increasingly to itself, pausing now and then for a jibe or two at modern man, usually taking an untenable position in jousting with the gods of the secular world (Bishop Samuel Wilberforce debating Charles Darwin in England and the "Scopes Monkey Trial" in America), or by mid-twentieth century, reconstructing repristination theology. Serious dialog did not develop between Christian and secular people in the·first half of the twentieth century.

The disciples of Nietzsche, Marx, Freud, Darwin, Spencer, and Einstein increased in numbers and influence in the disintegrating Christian culture of the West. Their vigorous critiques of dogma, man, and society, coupled with their philosophic and pragmatic remedies, fell on the fertile soil of a rapidly deteriorating historical situation. Two devasting world wars, an enervating economic depression that shook the social foundations of the industrial nations, the advent of nuclear weapons powerful enough to obliterate entire metropolises, Asia in ferment, Africa in revolt, Latin America in turmoil, the Middle East employing the exploitative practices once used on them by Europe and the United States, "triage" thinking as a viable response to mass starvation, and galloping inflation[18]—all this disheartened and, in some quarters, overwhelmed the institutional church. Its preaching failed to keep pace with radical cultural changes. Its members—ordained ministers among them—came to terms with the world, took leave of institutional Christianity, or retreated into obscurantism, privatism, nostalgia, and narcissism.

The twentieth-century church—especially in Europe, North America, and Latin America—is part of the current social-moral problem. First, it let go of its biblical insights into the nature of God, the person, and society which had been forged over seventeen centuries of witness. Next, it handled God's moral commands rigidly, denying the ambiguities of modern life, or accommodated his demands to an increasingly amoral society, reducing them to shallow moralism. Finally, the church proclaimed God's gracious promises without ethical content for persons and society ("cheap grace") or espoused a brand of fundamentalism (anti-intellectual, obscurantist) that was compatible with the extreme right in American politics in the 1950s and 1960s.[19] Both these stances alienated people who were striving desperately to be human *and* to reshape the institutions of society to serve human needs.

Today, large segments of the formally educated community in the Americas and Western Europe, as well as millions of disillusioned uneducated people, are convinced that the Christian message is obsolete. Schleiermacher's nineteenth-century band of "cultured despisers" has burgeoned into a mighty army. The evangelistic thrust of the Christian church, which has fallen behind the population explosion, is being challenged by revolutionary governments and other religions—especially the religion of Islam in the Middle East, and Marxism in Africa, Asia, and Latin America. Presently, hosts of spiritually displaced persons populate the one-time Christian countries. Protestant and Roman Catholic congregations in Western Europe and North and South America are themselves primary mission fields. At the close of the nineteenth century a perceptive churchman, Marcus Dods, looking at the church in the world, observed, "I do not envy those who will carry the banner of Christianity in the twentieth century. . . . Yes, perhaps I do, but it will be a stiff fight." The fight has been stiffer than Dods predicted. It will get stiffer in the decades ahead because so many old chickens have come home to roost. A new age is aborning. It may be a Dark Age. Certainly all social institutions (family, education, state, and church) in the West are being found wanting.

In 1970, Thor Hall, then professor of preaching at Duke Divinity School, declared flatly that "there are few good sermons anymore. "Most sermons," he said, "carry the unmistakable marks of centuries of ecclesiastical and theological inbreeding. . . . The only sustenance they offer along the way is the condensed fears of past sentimentalists or the moldy paradoxes left by generations that passed this way before." [20] Although Hall's judgment is still true in many pulpits, Donald McLeod, professor of preaching at Princeton Theological Seminary, judged a decade later "that the students there, especially the women, were more serious about biblical preaching—and doing it better—than the students in the 1960s and early 1970s." [21] The tide may be turning slowly as the church enters the closing decades of the twentieth century. Certainly, a minority knows that if biblical preaching were to die, so would the church. "Preaching founded it, carried it to the far corners of the earth and has sustained it in existence, battered, diminished, and humbled as it may be, to this day." [22] The early Christians, as T. R. Glover observed, out-loved, out-gave, and out-died the devotees of the pagan religions in the early Christian centuries.

That did not occur because professional evangelists, church functionaries, and public officials called piously for church renewal, or mission, or a religious revival. It occurred because Paul and Peter, Phoebe and Timothy, Tertullian and Chrysostom preached Christ crucified, raised from the dead, victoriously alive in the world.

When this generation of parish pastors argues that clergy in earlier centuries preached in less demanding cultural settings, they may be right. But a realistic reading of life in the early church during the twilight of Greco-Roman culture and the steady advance of the barbarians, or of life in sixteenth-century Europe when a new worldview was emerging and strife between and among Christians was rife reveals that preaching in both eras was intensely demanding, frustrating, and exhausting. When present day ministers are convinced that God's Word in the human activity of preaching is his power to refashion persons who, equipped from and sustained by that Word, will work to transform their culture, they stand in the direct line of the apostles and the prophets. The biblical preacher in any era has confidence in the human activities of preaching and teaching because he or she has learned to have confidence in the Word itself.

In the next chapter we shall examine some of the problems inherent in discerning God's Word in the human words fashioned by men and women in different eras and cultures, who, prompted by the Holy Spirit, gave the church its primary authority—the Holy Scriptures.

2 Preaching in Today's Theological Context

The time for fairy tales is past.
> —Schleiermacher to the cultured despisers of the faith

Blessed Lord, by whose providence all holy Scriptures were written and preserved for our instruction, give us grace to study them this and every day, with patience and love. . . . Strengthen our souls with the fullness of their divine teaching.
> —B. F. Westcott's prayer before studying the Bible

GOD'S HERALDS IN THE WANING YEARS of the twentieth century carry the same double burden that Amos and Isaiah, Hosea and Micah carried in the eighth century B.C. They must be able to hear both the whisperings and thunderings of God's Spirit; and, at the same time, they must be able to discern the signs of the times. Even the most sensitive proclamation of God's Word will be only partially effective if the preacher is ignorant of the historical *and* theological context from which, as well as in which, his words are spoken.

Today's theological context has its own peculiar forms of the old familiar enemies: sin, a pernicious brand of

39

moral decline, and disrespect and disregard for God's authority with all the attendant symptoms of formless fear, crippling anxiety, craven accommodation, and lack of personal and communal discipline. Only a clear understanding and personal acceptance of God's authority in and through the Scriptures can equip today's preachers to recognize these signs and speak persuasively the Word that liberates persons, themselves among them, from a liberty that has become license.

Preaching in the closing decades of the twentieth century is not, we have observed, an easy affair. Americans inside and outside the church entertain a shallow view of sin. In spite of the horrors of the twentieth century, they evidence little awareness of the streak of insanity that runs through the history of the human species. They seem not to sense that something is dreadfully wrong with human nature. They do not appear to understand the schizophrenic Western mind that produced "the splendors of our cathedrals . . . . and the gargoyles that decorate them." [1] Their desperate need for Divine rescue is barely perceived. Sin stains those who go to church and those who never enter its doors. It smothers persons in self-interest, fractures human relationships, and, institutionalized, oppresses millions of people. Consequently, creativity is destroyed by a mechanical methodology. Innovation is crowded out by prefabricated thought. Growth through personal confrontation and serious dialog is throttled by "process thinking," "encounter" groups, and "committee" decisions. Orwell's *1984* appears to be on schedule! Values that once seemed right to the majority of church people—and were unassailable in Western society—have been shaken, shattered, and obliterated since 1914. America's moral center is disintegrating.

Not only the authority of God but authority in any

guise is anathema to most Americans. Three perceptive European historians—deTocqueville, Bryce, and Brogan—assessing the American mind at half-century intervals, documented this cutural fault. At mid-twentieth century, an American historian, Henry Steele Commager, appraised the American citizen in this blunt fashion: "Two world wars had not induced in him either a sense of sin or that awareness of evil almost instinctive with most Old World peoples. . . . War had not taught him discipline or respect for authority." [2] But the Americans' revolt against God's authority was underway as far back as 1760. Edmund S. Morgan, Sterling Professor of American History at Yale University, writes: "The Puritan Ethic as it existed among the Revolutionary generation had in fact lost for most men the endorsement of an omni-present angry God. The element of divinity had not entirely departed, but it was a good deal diluted." [3] Secular American society and civil religion, born in the last quarter of the eighteenth century, came to maturity in the twentieth century.

Until God's authority is recognized, acknowledged, and acted on *in local congregations,* there can be no revival of the church nor renewal of the nation. [4] The first can come, and perhaps the second, only with a revival of biblical preaching and evangelical teaching in tens of thousands of congregations *and* their consequent deeds of servanthood in society. It is God's Spirit, through the preaching and teaching of his Word, who raises up witnesses to and doers of his Word. But persons must accept God's authority if that is to occur. Obviously, until the church—Protestant, Roman Catholic, Orthodox—learns to respect God's authority, accepts it, and endeavors seriously to live under it, the institutional church will not get a serious hearing in our undisciplined secular society.

All Protestants agree formally on the seat of authority: *sola scriptura.* But modern day Protestants understand better than their spiritual fathers why their Roman Cath-·olic colleagues are engulfed presently in controversy over the issue of authority: Scripture and/or tradition. At the grass roots, Protestants face a similar dilemma on four levels:

1. unbiblical denominational-sectarian traditions,
2. uncertainty over the historical relationship between the Scriptures and the Word of God,
3. the place of critical scholarship in the local congregation, and
4. the social-political implications of the scriptural witness to God's mighty deeds. Only in a few congregations have the clergy worked diligently to teach lay people the meaning of revelation, the nature of the Bible, and the differing literary forms that bear witness to God's progressive self-revelation.

Presently, all church bodies are confused more or less, and some rent asunder, over the nature and authority of the Scriptures. Is the Bible the Word of God, or does it contain the Word of God, or is it both? How are revelation and history related? How does God speak today? Wide differences exist among Protestant, Roman Catholic, and Orthodox laity on these questions. How lay people perceive, understand, and do God's Word depends substantially on the church's teaching office, a primary function of the ordained ministry. Ordained clergy, set apart by the several churches to minister full-time to lay people, are the chief teachers of the church. They are the stated preachers, theologians-in-residence, and pastoral leaders of the congregations. Unfortunately, too many ordained ministers, appointed to be shepherds who guide and care for people from the resources of God's Word, turn out to be sheep dogs that do their earthly master's bidding.[5] Others are too confused to preach the Word boldly and teach it concretely.

The thesis to be developed in this chapter is this. What a particular preacher believes about the relationship between the Bible and the Word of God (how he or she views revelation and history) determines the content, structure, and style of his or her preaching. If Pastor Richard Smith believes in the literal inspiration of the Scriptures, his view of the Scriptures will affect not only what he preaches but how he preaches. In the extreme, he may use the "Word" like a blunt instrument to intimidate his hearers. If the Rev. Janice Jones is persuaded that divine revelation appears in the Scriptures in propositional forms, her preaching will take the form of statements of doctrine to which she expects her hearers to give intellectual assent. If the Rev. Joseph Williams demythologizes all Scripture, he will frustrate his hearers' need to anchor their faith in the historical Jesus. His preaching will separate revelation from history. Preaching that begins in experience but never gets into the Bible as the record of God's self-revelation is not biblical. Preaching that imprisons Christ in the Bible or caricatures him in theological propositions is not biblical, either. What the preacher believes about *inspiration* and *revelation* makes a particular form of sermon inevitable.[6]

No pastor can preach biblically until he or she discerns for himself or herself how divine truth is communicated to human beings through the biblical record. Consequently, the preacher's "working" doctrine of the Word determines how he or she proclaims God's truth. Accordingly, his or her approach becomes authoritarian, propositional, open-ended, based on value judgments, or confrontation-

al-in-freedom. Those preachers who do not accept the
literal inspiration in the Scriptures must establish intelligibly for themselves *and* for their congregations the relationship between God's self-revelation (the Divine
Word) in history and the Spirit-prompted human language in which it is set down in the Scriptures. Those
preachers who do accept verbal inspiration must defend
their doctrine of the Word in the light of biblical criticism
and in the arena of a technological culture. R. E. C.
Browne observes that to take any one of the several positions on inspiration "provokes questions which must be
considered—christological questions and questions which
concern beliefs about the nature of the ceaseless activity
of God without which there could be no thought or
speech." [7] Then he goes to the heart of it:

> If the biblical writers were automatic writers who
> transcribed at the divine dictation, then the preacher
> must look on his work in the same light. If the biblical
> writers are held to be free agents who used their imagi-
> nation and intelligence in obedience to the divine
> promptings to say the greatest things about God and
> man, then the preacher must look on his work accord-
> ingly. Only thus may the preacher discover more clearly
> the nature of the creative effort he is to make in his
> work with words. [8]

The biblical preacher does not avoid the problems historical, psychological, sociological, and scientific criticism
have posed for the Christian faith. "The time for fairy
tales is past"; revelational theology must stand on its own.

Every preacher is morally bound to clarify his or her
view on the nature and authority of the Scriptures and
to act out that critical understanding in all facets of parish ministry, in his or her personal and family life, and
as a responsible citizen. When the clergy fail to do this,

they confuse or divide the congregations they serve, confuse or divide their families, and develop a degree of schizophrenia or hypocrisy in their own persons. An elemental strand in the complex problem of preaching in this era is that so many preachers simply do not know by whose authority they preach. Biblical preaching depends first on the preacher's ability in the strength of God's Spirit to discern his Word in the Spirit-prompted words of his human servants in earlier centuries (Bible), to accept that authority, to interpret it in the context of the church's history, and to communicate it intelligibly and persuasively through his or her preaching, teaching, counseling, *and* person to other persons who are free to accept or reject God's Word. Acceptance of his Word is acceptance of his authority. Jesus' question, "Why call me Lord, and do not my commandments?" provides an essential focus for serious Christians in any era.

One of the church's primary services to God and the world is its responsible custodianship of biblical truth through its willingness to accept God's authority. If that custodianship—which depends largely on the preaching-teaching ministry of the congregation—goes, the church goes, too. Paul perceived and taught that God calls all Christians to be responsible stewards of the mysteries of the gospel. How a church discerns the Word of God couched in the Spirit-prompted human language of the Scriptures, how it defines the relationship between the Word and the Bible, how it understands revelation and history, how it perceives and accepts God's authority, and how it applies his Word in concrete situations determine whether that church gets God's life-giving message into a dying world. How a particular preacher handles these tasks determines the substance and style of his or her preaching, his or her identity as a Christian person, and his or her effectiveness as a minister of Christ. The Roman Catholic theologian, Karl Rahner, has properly reminded the whole church that "the knowledge and experience of the living God is not a privilege of the clergy."[9] Essentially, that is what the Reformers expressed in their concept of the priesthood of believers: every Christian is a minister of Christ *under the authority of God's Word.* The Bible is the church's book. The Scriptures and the church are inseparable.

Mainline Protestant churches agree substantially that the Word of God is the good news of God's saving work in Christ. They accept it as the message about the essential nature and purpose of God's dynamic, saving activity initiated at creation and revealed by Spirit-prompted humans, and preeminently revealed in the historical person of Jesus of Nazareth. Scripture is the personal-corporate record of Spirit-prompted human witness to God's saving activity in history. Authentic religious experience, part of human history, testifies to his saving activity. How could it be otherwise? We are not "souls with ears." We are flesh and blood mortals. We exist in time.

Mainline Protestant denominations also argue that the key to interpreting all Scripture is Christ. That was Luther's stance: "If the scriptures themselves, as a whole, claim to be the Word of God, they can be that only if they are, as a whole, interpreted in terms of Christ. . . . Christ is Lord of the scriptures."[10] The biblical account of God's saving activity is more than a report. The Christ event, rooted in an identifiable moment of history (Barth), is not bound by history (Bultmann). The Christ event is historical and existential. Since God reveals himself *in* history, revelation should be viewed *as* God acting in history (Pannenberg).

Biblical scholarship exists to help the church preach

and teach the whole counsel of God. If scholarship is to be an aid rather than a hindrance, a unifying force rather than a divisive one, it must find a solid place in the congregation's teaching ministry. The ordained minister is the scholar, the theologian-in-residence, the chief teacher. The pulpit, church school classes, and study groups can be employed to equip lay persons to *discern* God's Word in the Bible. Biblical scholarship is not bound by Protestant, Roman Catholic, Orthodox, or sectarian traditions. It seeks to discern the divine Word in the human words, Spirit-prompted certainly, but human nonetheless, even as Jesus was human as well as divine. Each congregation should be a teaching community where all its members learn how to discern God's Word in the Scriptures. Biblical preachers accept this magisterial office as eagerly as Luther and Calvin and John XXIII did. They know who they are—shepherds, prophets, pastors, priests, teachers, and theologians.

One evidence that a pastor is a servant of the Word is his or her effort to persuade the congregation to exercise its evangelical teaching ministry seriously rather than blindly or mechanically. The clergy are not the only teachers. Lay people are called to the office of teaching, too. The primary responsibility of the lay leaders elected to the official board, for example, is not administrative but biblical and theological: to see that the Word of God is rightly preached and taught by the full-time minister(s) and the appointed lay ministers, and that persons elected to lead the congregation are not chosen because they are loyal to old "First Church" or because their position in the community is notable, but because their commitment to and knowledge of Jesus Christ is maturing. Until the congregation is equipped to discern the Word in the Scriptures, and proclaim and teach it responsibly, Jesus will be imprisoned in a book, obscured by the mists of value judgments, or presented as a "model" for all kinds of human ventures. Lay people must be challenged, motivated, and equipped to discern, explore, and proclaim the fundamental article of the Christian Faith: "God was in Christ reconciling the world unto himself."[11]

Critical scholarship, employed at the congregational level, enables the church to identify and understand the varied historical contexts and literary forms in which God's mighty deeds were accomplished and communicated, since many *were* the ways and forms in which God spoke to our fathers. Pluralism (worship, Christology, images of the church, varieties of Christian experience, and so on) is a dominant characteristic of the Old and New Testaments. Biblical preaching requires that the preacher establish the original meaning of a biblical text or passage wherever that is possible and communicate its existential meaning to "Protean man" in concrete contemporary images. Exegesis, interpretation, and application are strands in biblical preaching. "The sermon which starts in the Bible and stays in the Bible is not biblical." Neither is the sermon that starts in the world and never gets into the Bible.

The teaching office of the Christian ministry, responsibly exercised, guards against the limitations inherent in demythologization and symbolism. It guards against literalism and moralism. It also provides a solid perspective for evaluating and appreciating charismatic gifts. Extensive demythologizing of the New Testament can lead a pastor and congregation to lose Christ and his message in the fog of value judgments. Literalism can lead a pastor and congregation to imprison Christ in a book, devaluing his message. Charismatic gifts, accepted uncritically by pastor and congregation, can obscure Christ by focusing on the charismatic individuals, especially their particular religious experiences.

The Scriptures must be allowed to speak their sovereign message objectively to a needy world in images that are readily understood by modern listeners. But this is likely to occur powerfully only in congregations with ministers who use the tools of biblical scholarship to discern the divine Word in the Spirit-prompted human language of the Bible, proclaim it, *and* teach their people how to use these tools to discern the Word for themselves.

A word of caution. Biblical scholarship is a tool, a means for discerning God's Word. *It is not a new authority*. When one takes the position that God's self-revelation occurred and continues to occur *in* history (not above or outside history), he or she has a new view: God's revelation is history. It is history happening. The Christian use of historical criticism then is not bound to a positivistic historicism.[12] Alan Richardson put this succinctly: "It is an occupational idiosyncrasy of professional Biblical scholars to imagine that Christian Faith rests upon their ability or inability to solve the historical problems that are raised by it. It does not. It rests upon the testimony of a people." [13] But the substantial results of biblical and historical criticism—and of the natural and social sciences—cannot be blotted from people's minds today. We preach to people who have a radically different attitude toward the Scriptures from their forbears in the sixteenth, thirteenth, or first century. This affects their view of the Bible in general and revelation in particular.

Christians believe in the Scriptures because of Christ. The early church was born under the preaching of Christ crucified and raised from the dead and the teaching of his ethic. From this oral tradition of preaching and teaching, the early church produced the gospels and epistles and the apocalypse of John, accepted the writings of the Old Testament, and by the fourth century had established the canon as we know it today. Correlatively, Christians believe in Christ because of the Spirit-prompted biblical record. Without the written word, both preaching and teaching would have died with the third and fourth generations of Christians. Without the Spirit-prompted written record, Christ would be lost in the distant past. Luther put it well when he said that holy writ is the manger in which Christ is laid. Scripture is the church's primary authority, but that authority is weakened, its impact deflected, its demands blunted, and its good news distorted unless Christ's lordship over the Scriptures is recognized, acknowledged, and acted on. Jerome observed late in the fourth century, "Ignorance of the Scriptures is ignorance of Christ." It is equally true that unless one accepts the lordship of Christ over the Scriptures he or she cannot clearly understand the Bible's witness to God's mighty deeds.

Christ is the key to interpreting all Scripture reliably. But a responsible custodianship of the Word-Event also sees to it that Jesus Christ—God the Redeemer—is not split from God the Creator of the natural world and the human family and God the Spirit who acts in our history as he acted in biblical times. This Trinitarian view rescues scripture from the murky swamps of existentialism, the dungeons of literalism, and the heresy of Socinianism. It does so because it accepts and works with history and faith, divine revelation and human response. This contextual view, historical and existential, guides pastors and people in discerning, preaching, and teaching God's full counsel. The Bible was not written above or outside history; it is the story of God's mighty acts in the world at particular times in concrete situations.

The sovereign, righteous, law-giving God of the Israelites is the patient, merciful, suffering servant (Isaiah 53)
whom the Christian church knows, loves, serves, and proclaims as Jesus of Nazareth, the resurrected Christ. There
is not a God of the Old Testament and a God of the New
Testament; and there is firm continuity from the historical
Jesus to the kerygmatic Christ. The God we know in the
resurrected Christ is the God of Abraham and Hosea,
John the Baptist, and Jesus of Nazareth. To preach only
from the New Testament or to preach from the Old Testament as though God had not come in Christ is to caricature God's Word. Either without the other is not biblical
preaching. The Exodus and the Resurrection are the focal
points in the scriptural witness to God's liberating deeds
in history. Christ is the absolute authority for interpreting all Scripture: "You have heard it said in the past . . .
but I tell you. . . ." He came to fulfill the moral law and
the prophets, not to destroy or to ignore them. Biblical
preaching is rooted in both Testaments. It is law and
gospel, demand and promise, judgment and grace. It
provides the points of contact "where past and future
meet in the fleeting brevity of the present; it is a sudden
illumination of human experience." [14] Biblical preaching
is not a bag of dead bones. It is a fresh, relevant interpretation in our era under the guidance of the Holy Spirit
of the faith once delivered to the prophets and the apostles.

Scripture, then, is the witness of human experience with
God at its center. God acted as he did in Old Testament
days because he would, in the fullness of time, do what
he did in Christ. Luther's suggestion that we should begin
with the sayings of Jesus makes sense: "Scripture begins
tenderly and leads us to Christ as a man, then to the Lord
over all creatures, and then to God." But he does not

suggest that Jesus' teachings are the whole Word of God. The church accepts all the canonical writings as the substantively inspired witness to God's ongoing self-revelation and mighty acts of liberation. One glaring weakness in the preaching of my generation is its cavalier dismissal of two thirds of God's revelation in history, the Old Testament. It is impossible to understand Jesus apart from the Word of God witnessed to by the Old Testament records which informed his mind and heart. The ancient heresy of Marcion, alive in today's pulpits, emasculates biblical preaching. Jesus said bluntly that if we do not understand Moses (God's moral law) we cannot understand him. He did not abrogate God's law; he fulfilled it.

Biblical preaching also recognizes that God's self-revelation is not an idea to be fondled or debated forensically. It represents in fact the past, present, and future activities of God that are to be discerned, proclaimed, heard, acknowledged, and acted on. Anders Nygren observes that "the Bible is the message about this continuing action. But this message is itself an action of God." When God's Word is discerned, preached, heard, and responded to, his action occurs in and through those persons in a particular place at a specific time. When Martin Luther King, Jr., spoke out against racism in Montgomery, Alabama in 1954, he stepped into the line of the prophets, the apostles, and Jesus himself. The kerygmatic Christ appealed to this generation in and through that particular black Baptist preacher to repent, believe, and follow him in the world. The message of Christ, Luther observed, is not "an old song about an event that happened fifteen-hundred years ago. . . . It is a gift and bestowing that endures forever." The Christ event, rooted in history, is not bound by past history; it continues to work in *our* history. Biblical preachers, understanding this, seek to get "Protean man" to understand it, confident that God's Word is working in their personal proclamation of it.

The resurrection of Jesus is more than a spiritual high and more than a resuscitated corpse. Understanding *that* affirms the historical event yet transcends history, placing those who name the name of Jesus squarely in the realm of God's kingdom while they are still in this world. Revelation *is* history. The apostles knew this in the upper room when the doors were shut and the resurrected Christ appeared. Paul knew this when the resurrected Christ confronted him on the Damascus road. Christians are assured and strengthened by this reality each day of their lives.

To the eyes of faith, the resurrection of Jesus is a cosmic event in which time and eternity meet, where God brings the beginnings of a new creation to a world ripped apart by sin, shackled by guilt, and defeated by death. It is an event as historical (it really happened in a particular moment of time) yet more mysterious and awe-inspiring than that "moment" billions of years ago when the nucleotides and amino acids in the oceans of a lifeless planet were made alive. God created life, and the cosmos (heaven and earth) became the active expression of his creative love. God's resurrection of Jesus is the beginning of a *new* "natural" creation and, since that event, neither humanity nor the world can ever be the same again. To be sure, the coming of God's kingdom in Jesus of Nazareth and in the resurrected Christ were not significant events *in that time and world,* yet they set an end to both. The new world of God is already at work.[15] I do not know what other planets God has visited or will visit, but the evidence is clear that he was on earth in the person of

Jesus in the days of Caesar Augustus.[16] I accept readily
that he died for me. I believe that God raised Jesus from
the dead. I know that the resurrected Christ has found
me and ushered me into a new life. I trust that he, having begun a good work in me, will bring it to completion.
I am persuaded that he has called me to tell his story to
others. I know that he equips and enables not only me but
all persons whom he calls to do his work in and through
his Son's church in the world. I am persuaded that he will
come one day, in God's "time," in all his power and glory.

In the deepest sense then, I believe the biblical account. Critically, I view the resurrection as the supreme
event in human history. In testifying to Jesus' bodily
resurrection, I testify to God's power in raising Jesus from
the dead and his continuing power to renew persons
through the resurrected Christ. It is, therefore, to me, as
it was to Paul and millions of Christians over the centuries, the historical event that is the cornerstone of the
good news and the church, because it is God's validation
of Jesus' person and teaching. "We do not follow cun-
ningly devised fables" (1 Peter 1:16). I do not preach
a Christ lost in a maze of subjectivism or bound hand and
foot to the Bible or immobilized by an unbiblical doctrine. It is because of that Word event, preached and
heard, remembered and celebrated, that I know that my
Redeemer lives; recognize him in preaching and teaching
and sacraments and in all hurting humanity; obey him
trustfully here and now; and look confidently to his vic-
torious return. Emil Brunner, acknowledging his debt to
Kierkegaard and attempting to correct Karl Barth's preoccupation with biblical texts, put it lucidly:

> To know him (i.e. God) in trustful obedience is not
> only to know the truth, but through God's self-communi-
> cation to *be* in it, in the truth that as love is at the same

time fellowship. The truth about man is founded in the
divine humanity of Christ, which we apprehend in faith
in Christ, the Word of God. This is truth as encounter.[17]

The intention of preaching, Charles Rice asserts, "is
to bring men to . . . an encounter with God. In the event
of preaching, men face the ultimate questions." [18] Encounter with the trinitarian God is biblical preaching.
Jesus of Nazareth, whom we learn to know in the biblical records, is the resurrected Christ whom we recognize
in his church and in God's world today. The God who
created our first parents created us. His Spirit, who led
the Israelites from bondage and by whose power the
prophets and apostles spoke, calls, enlightens, and empowers us. Biblical preachers teach their congregations
the *critical* as well as the devotional use of the Bible,
engage them in theological conversations, encourage them
to take the leap of faith, help them to fashion risk-taking
ministries in their respective communities to test for themselves whether God's story is true, and support them in
their expectation that ultimate victory is God's gift to
Christ's co-workers.

The Scriptures are like the flesh and blood in which
God came into history as a human being. They are the
inspired written remembrances of God's self-revelation
inside human experience—history. The church believes
the Bible because it believes in Christ; and it believes
in Christ because it believes the Bible is the Spirit-prompted human record of God's mighty acts in history. There
would be no faith in God through Christ today, and the
life of Jesus would be a forgotten event or one dimly remembered in the world's history if the record had not
been committed to writing and preserved by people who
were prompted by God's Spirit. "The New Testament

contains the deposit, in writing, of the continuous tradition about Jesus at various stages of its transmission during the first century of the church's existence." [19] The whole Bible is the church's book, the story of the God of Abraham and Jesus *remembered, honored,* and *served* in the oldest surviving society in the Western world—the holy, catholic church.

In effective biblical preaching, the Holy Spirit works mediately through God's Word *and* the human messenger of that Word. "Scripture itself, then, creates the need for preachers" who will accept Christ's call to assemble "believing communities, address them in the name and power of the Lord Jesus, and act as his prophets. Along with Scripture, the evangelical preacher is constitutive to apostolic presence." [20] Biblical preaching is God's continuing action (revelation) in our human experience.

It is the living Word then, Christ himself, who is the preacher's authority because it is the church's authority. How his authority claims persons and constrains them to preach is the theme of the next chapter. Without God's authority, preaching is both presumptuous and ineffective.

3 The Preacher's Call and Office

> There in Babylonia beside the Cheba River, I heard the Lord speak to me and I felt his power.
> —Ezekiel 1:3

> When I saw this, I fell face downward on the ground. Then I heard a voice saying, "Mortal man, stand up. I want to talk to you." While the voice was speaking, God's Spirit entered me and raised me to my feet, and I heard the voice continue, "Mortal man, I am sending you to the people of Israel. They have rebelled and turned against me and are still rebels, just as their ancestors were."
> —Ezekiel 2:1-3a

THE QUESTION, "WHO DARES TO PREACH?" haunts the preacher in his first year of preaching and every year thereafter. Gardner C. Taylor goes to the heart of the problem: "Measured by almost any gauge, preaching is a presumptuous business." [1] Who are we—a handful of men and women no different in our human frailties from those to whom we preach and decidedly less "good" and certainly less talented than some to whom we preach—to presume to preach to them or anyone? If too few clergy ask this question of themselves, lay people are not gentle in asking it, especially when the preacher challenges *their* life-style, political judgments, racial prejudices, and economic interests. Secular people outside the church also ask the question when their self-interest is at stake. Biblical preachers ask it of themselves throughout their full-time ministries.

Every generation has ministers who preach, as some did in Paul's day, under constraints other than those laid on them by God. Some in this generation still see the ministry as a refuge from the harsh pressures of a competitive society. Others look on it as a career less demanding in preparation and performance than a career in medicine or law, business or teaching. Still others enter for reasons that would surface only in long-term psychoanalysis. Because of God's grace, human freedom, and the human capacity to grow, some of these men and women are called in due season and become useful to Christ. Phillips Brooks, only after having failed as a teacher, turned to the ministry. Frederick Robertson, only after failing to get an appoinment to Sandhurst, the English West Point, turned to the Christian ministry. Brooks and Robertson were two of the ablest biblical preachers in the nineteenth century. God is willing to use failures—all of us at one time or other—to do his work effectively. In time many of these come under a powerful inner constraint (call) to preach; they become profitable to the gospel. Those who are experienced in Christ's ministry need to be more patient with young candidates who are idealistic rather than realistic about God's work. Few of us reached our present level of knowledge and commitment without severe frustrations, searing failures, and anguished hours of prayer.

Everyone who proclaims the Word is fulfilling certain felt or unconscious needs—as is the doctor, school teacher, lawyer, business executive, and others. This is in the nature of being mortal, an earthen vessel. It need not be an occasion for guilt. It is in the purpose of God to speak his Word through human words; he uses those peculiar constraints that are embedded in his spokespersons. Paul's thorn in the flesh, Luther's penchant for controversy, King's charismatic personality were useful to God in getting his Word preached effectively in the first, sixteenth, and twentieth centuries.

No preacher has a call that he or she has not tarnished, but every authentic preacher had initially or comes to know a deep sense of personal call from God. From the first disciples of Jesus to the present generation, men and women have been chosen, called, commissioned, and entrusted with the gospel by Christ himself. Spirit speaks to spirit. Certainly one distinguishing mark of "called" ministers is that they do not *choose* to preach; they are singled out and sent under orders. God got to them by closing doors (Phillips Brooks and Frederick Robertson), hounding them (Francis Thompson), showing them the needs of human beings (William Temple), blocking their way in another pursuit (Paul), making them dissatisfied with a secure but dull economic future (Moses), destroying the base of a life-long security (Isaiah), setting them at odds with their neighbors' perception of reality (Ezekiel). Like Jeremiah, some ask to the end of their days, "Why me?" But they are constrained to preach: "Woe is me, if I preach not the gospel. . . ." Those who escape this inner tension or manage to ease it are not Christ's co-workers. Jeremiah called them false prophets. Jesus called them hirelings. H. H. Farmer called them professionals. Today, some call them careerists.

Biblical preachers are not self-appointed. They are called by God through Christ's church. They are not simply "recruited" by the institutional church which must

become more critical (evaluative) as well as compassionate (caring) in examining the prospective preacher's
personal call (inner sense of divine constraint, commitment to Christ, sense of urgency to preach) and his or
her *providential* call (talents, emotional health, personality, social sensitivity, and academic credentials). The institutional church must learn again to challenge its candidates for the ministry. Jesus told his disciples plainly
that a cross would fall to each of them if they followed
him. To be sure, those often dazed first disciples did not
fully understand what he told them, but when severe
hardships and martyrdom came they had a frame of
reference for accepting and handling both as well as the
support of Christ himself.

Candid, sensitive, concrete discussions of the candidate's personal call with other experienced, perceptive,
compassionate Christians can be helpful to him or her.
Jesus made it plain that the servant of the Word is not
above his or her Master. The church must get that truth
to its candidates. Any preacher who is not willing to struggle to become a servant of the Word, however gifted
personally and qualified academically, is not called by
God. In-depth dialogs with each candidate about the nature and purpose of biblical ministry—and his or her
personal call—are a pressing need in the church today.
Presently, the church relies too much on psychological
testing and too little on the Christian insights and perceptions of its own experienced clergy and mature laity.
Consequently, it ordains too many men and women who
set out to become "professionals." These careerists, not
ministers of the Word, use the church bureaucracy to
advance themselves.

Men and women who want to learn and grow as Christian ministers discover quickly that biblical ministry in

any parish demands significant spiritual growth on their part before they can, as collaborators with Christ, persuade parishioners to be collaborators too in the renewal of their parishes. Pastors and people need to recognize that both are part of the moral problem (what is true?), and that both suffer the same identity crisis (what does it mean to be truly human in the contemporary world?).

> The issue is not if the laity were only given the opportunity and the right to do so, they would come to the rescue of the Church. The issue is that both laity and ministry stand in need of a new vision of the nature and calling of the Church and their *distinctive places* in it, which means conversion and reformation of the whole Church, laity as well as ministry.[2]

But what image of ministry is authentic? Augustine in the fourth century appears to have been authoritarian and directive in administering the church. The parish priest in the late fifteenth and early sixteenth centuries was a mechanical administrant of the seven sacraments, a dispenser of earned grace. The preacher emerged as the strong figure during the Reformation. The counselor was sought after in the age of pietism. The pulpit personality reigned in late nineteenth century England and the United States. The social gospeler was the dramatic figure prior to the First World War. After World War II, the image of the pastoral director became dominant in parish life, although the older conceptions—the preacher, the teacher, the priest—still flourished.[3] The pastoral director of the 1950s became the administrator-manager in the 1960s and the "professional enabler" in the 1970s.

Presently, some argue that the minister is effective if and when he is a "professional."[4] This concept of the ministry as a *profession* is a thoroughly modern view; it is framed by our technological culture. "It focuses around the concept of technical competence, and partakes of the modern period with its practical concerns, its Cartesian theory of knowledge ('it is not what I am but what I have and what I do with it that counts'), and its middle-class commitment to work and duty . . . all other professionals are expected to be in control of their areas of competence." [5] But the pastor-preacher is *not* in control. God's Word does what God wills, not what the preacher wills. Indeed, human freedom is not "controlled" by God himself. He wants sons and daughters, not slaves. Skills in preaching, teaching, counseling, and liturgical leadership are learned from teachers, reading, and experience—and they are important. But it is the new creature in Christ who receives through faith those charismatic gifts apart from which the ministry of Christ is not accomplished however competent—"professional"—the preacher may be. If the minister is committed to an image of personhood and ministry fashioned by culture, sect, flashy talent, or unbridled pride, he or she may achieve a measure of success, but only at high cost to his person and Christ's ministry.

Pastors and lay people need to search the Scriptures critically and through them allow the Holy Spirit to fashion an authentic image of ministry testing it daily in private and public life until it pervades their life-style. The Word of God in its offense and healing is the essential and informing substance and strength of authentic ministry. The specific forms that authentic ministry employs vary from culture to culture and from congregation to congregation in the same culture, but at its core biblical ministry rests on the Word confronting persons through persons in the context of human freedom. This is the image that emerges from the Scriptures.

God feeds and provides for the flock of Israel, appoints persons to exercise his ministry, and holds each appointed custodian accountable for the welfare of those entrusted to him (2 Kings 22:17; Jer. 3:15; and Ezek. 34:2). He chastises careless shepherds for neglecting their flocks and allowing them to be scattered (Jer. 2:8; 23:1-4; 5;4). He rebukes selfish shepherds who use their flocks to further their personal interests (Ezek. 34:10). In the third chapter of Ezekiel, the shepherd emerges as God's bold prophet who is answerable only to God who appointed and sent him. The prophet (God's messenger) listens eagerly each day for God's Word to undergird and strengthen the people committed to his or her care. In Second Isaiah (50:4-11), the prophet perceives that he strengthens the flock only when God's truth confronts and comforts people through his person.

Every preacher's primary responsibility then is fidelity to God's Word. This may sound cold and impersonal to religious "enthusiasts," but it is biblical. God's gifts of peace and power come at high cost to the human ego. Self-discipline and servanthood are at the heart of biblical faith. J. W. Stevenson, writing about his first parish in Scotland, points to the right relationship between God's ministers and their people: "If we look for the kind of preaching which will leave us as we are, we shall find that it is not to bring that kind of peace that Christ has come but with a sword to pierce it. . . . The true Church is the fellowship of people in whom the old human life is breaking down and the new life in Christ is being formed." [6] The first test of biblical ministry then is *fidelity* to God's Word. To preach Christ is to love God's truth, and to love his people too. Truth without love crushes the human spirit; love without truth emaciates it.

Jesus accepted, fulfilled, and enlarged the biblical picture of ministry that emerged from Israel's custodianship of God's self-disclosure in creation, deliverance, law, and the prophets. When Jesus spoke of the hireling who flees the endangered flock and identified himself as the Good Shepherd (John 10:11-17), he was not fashioning a new image of ministry; he was orienting to and enlarging an ancient one. Demonstrating that the prophet is one who speaks for God at all costs, Jesus, fulfilling the law and the prophets' teaching, set a collision course for Calvary. Obedient to the end ("My God, why . . . . ?") and interceding for humanity ("Father, forgive them. . . ."), he gave his life ("No man takes my life. . . .") to overmatch humanity's deep-set disposition to rebel against God. The church's embodiment and enactment of this suffering servant image is authentic ministry. The church exists to minister, not to be the object of ministry. It exists to expend its given life for the sake of the world. The church's called ministers, ordained and lay, are not above their Master.

This image was the "picture in the minds" of the apostles. Peter and John demonstrated and taught that Christ's ministers are called to please God rather than men (Acts 4:8-20), because that is in the best interests of all people. James, abhorring "cheap grace," taught that the good news and ethical instruction are inseparable (James 1 and 5). Paul, in his letter to the church in Rome, taught that the church exists to proclaim and teach Christ crucified, resurrected, victoriously present as crucial event *and* personal experience ("I know a man in Christ who fourteen years ago. . . ." 2 Cor. 12:2). There was nothing antiseptic about Paul's preaching.

The called minister then is any person in Christ who, knowing that he is cared for by the Shepherd as Bishop of his soul, cares for others from Christ's inexhaustible love. He and she recognize and accept that authentic ministry does not originate in the pastor's strong intellect, affable disposition, personal attractiveness, gregarious nature, or good digestive system. Authentic ministry centers in Christ. Shepherds care for people because Christ cares for them, motivating, and equipping them to care for others from his immeasurable love. They are enabled to speak God's truth in love to those who, like themselves, are free to accept or reject God's Word *and* its bearer.

The biblical evidence is that unless the God to whom one witnesses is allowed to incarnate himself in the person of the herald, the communication of Christ is limited, warped, sometimes aborted. Contemporary culture's preoccupation with communication as a matter of form more than of content and personhood reveals how severely "Protean man" is alienated from God, himself, and others. Kierkegaard is on target: "Where there is no God, there is no self." [7]

Surely we ought not consider our original authenticating call from God as invalid simply because it did not in a moment or a year transform us into mature disciples of the Lord Jesus Christ. However, no one has the right to continue in the ministry—nor can without harm to self, family, and congregation—unless he or she can say honestly, "How changed are my ambitions," and yearns to say, "For me to live is Christ."

Unless preachers wrestle daily with their own pride, sloth, acquisitiveness, lust, hostility, and envy in Christ's presence, they will not only abort their own growth in grace but also remain insensitive to the people in the pews every Sunday who themselves are struggling to realize Christ's call in *their* lives in the depersonalized climate of modern culture. Shepherd-prophets will not prostitute themselves to become pale copies of the cor-

poration team player hired to manage an institution or
to be professional enablers. They are alert to and resist
secular *and* ecclesiastical pressures to manipulate people
for the sake of an efficient institution.

Christ's messengers also learn that partial biblical
images—the *preacher,* the *priest,* the *pastoral counselor,*
the *teacher,* the *enabler,* the *administrator*—fragment the
church's ministry, because these images in practice exalt
one function of ministry above the others. These warped
images also tempt ministers to use one of these functions
of ministry to escape existential encounters with people
or to make their "speciality" a religious status symbol.
The preacher can loom so large that he stands between
the congregation and the Word of God; the priest can
become a specialist in liturgics; the counselor can become
a little tin god; the teacher can become an authority figure; the professional enabler can become a people manager; the administrator can become so efficient that the
institution hinders the work of the Spirit. This is what
Thor Hall is getting at when he writes:

> We are arguing for an inclusive concept of the min-
> istry of the Word, and not one that would separate the
> various ministrations in terms of limited and fragmented
> objectives. . . . The total ministry of the Word must be
> so conceived that each individual office is incorporated
> as integral to the church's ongoing confrontation with
> the gospel, and the individual ministrations of this
> Word-event must be so structured that the church can
> reap the full benefit of their peculiar capacity for facili-
> tating the confrontation with the constitutive Word as
> an ongoing reality in the life of the church.[8]

When the called minister seeks to lead his or her people
to take up Christ's ministry of preaching, teaching, healing, and social involvement, church members will inquire

about the place of the ordained minister. If every Christian is called to be a theologian, a pastor, a prophet, a teacher, an evangelist, a counselor, what need is there for a full-time ministry in the church? Is it not the responsibility of the ordained minister to preach and evangelize, teach and counsel? This is the inescapable "crunch" between the image of biblical ministry and the image of cultural ministry in our era. Mishandled, it thrusts pastor and people into adversary positions. Of course, there are other reasons why a minister and his or her congregation fall into adversary positions. Sometimes ministers and congregations are yoked unevenly. Too often the minister demands a leadership role simply on the grounds of his or her theological education and ordination, failing meantime to demonstrate leadership by his or her commitment to God and vocational competence. But in many congregations since 1960, lay people have frustrated, domesticated, or gotten rid of ministers who sought earnestly to do Christ's ministry and who *could have* if they had been given a decent chance. How then in this current "no man's land," does the pastor "lead" his or her congregation?

The called minister keeps in mind that the *office* of preaching, teaching, and the administration of the sacraments was instituted by God so that his Word might go out to all people. This ministry of the Word is not an order but an office, a function, a task to be performed. As a means of grace the ministry of the Word belongs to the whole church, the community of believers, with each believer called to bear witness to God's Word in deed and speech. This is the priesthood of believers. But a specially trained leadership is necessary. Martin Luther argued that we are all priests (lay ministers), but we are not all public ministers. Karl Barth's lifelong colleague, Eduard

Thurneysen, a parish pastor, put it this way: "It is the minister before others who has the credentials for pastoral care in that he is ordained and chosen as the shepherd of the congregation." [9]

We are all called to Christ's ministry in Holy Baptism, but we are not all *trained* theologians, preachers, teachers, and pastoral counselors. The full-time minister is the chief preacher, teacher, healer, and theologian-in-residence. That is his or her public ministry. This does not preclude the lay members from being preachers, teachers, healers, and theologians, too. Indeed, that is also their ministry, each according to his or her talents. Patiently, compassionately, firmly, the full-time minister leads lay people into this ministry, and, in due season, many parishioners are enabled by God's Spirit not only to minister to people in the world but also to support, correct, and prod him or her in doing Christ's ministry more responsibly. Together, pastor and people grow into *that* ministry. Initially, however, most parishioners need to be motivated, enlightened, equipped, and encouraged from the resources of God's Word (1 Peter 5:1-4). Shepherding is preeminently, but not exclusively, the ordained minister's task. All God's people are intended to be priests; but not all are intended to be ordained ministers. The pastor is the "lead actor" in the congregation; the lay people are the "lead actors" in the world.

Servants of the Word do not excuse their ignorance of far-reaching cultural problems, their ill-prepared preaching, and their shallow theology by pleading the press of parish duties or pushing programs for the national church —evasions which unconverted parishioners will accept as long as their pastor does not disturb their tight little world of self-interest. God's heralds are alert to the subtle and blatant pressures to accommodate his Word to the gods of modern culture, to the neurotic demands in the parish, and to the institutional demands of the church which occasionally run counter to God's intentions. Men and women who are God's messengers work diligently to understand the cultural situation in which the Word and its bearers must make their way. Like all earnest Christians, they nurture their new life in prayer, corporate worship, serious Bible study, and cultural awareness. They are haunted daily by Richard Baxter's warning to all preachers: "Beware, lest you be void of the saving grace that you offer to others."

Finally, we need to consider an aspect of this reality that is destructively peculiar, in strength and scope, to twentieth century people, including the sensitive preacher. This problem is more deep-seated than the cultural aversion to the gospel that we considered in chapter 1. It is an enervating boredom, a persuasion that the show is over. It is an emotional and volitional atrophy akin to what the medieval church called *accidie,* which can be interpreted in our day as a human response "in which there is a partial psychic paralysis." [10] Unless the clergy are sharply aware of this dimension that influences both themselves and their hearers, and unless they are also free enough of its hold over their own spirits, they will not preach biblically.

This dimension of our culture has been disturbingly focused by Professor Paul Jonas, an active participant in the ill-fated Hungarian Revolution in 1956, who, twenty years later assessed the hopes and dreams of that struggle from the perspective of "freedom" in the West. Like so many others who participated in that revolution, Professor Jonas was forced to flee his country or face execution. But he left Hungary with the hope of carrying on the revolutionary cause from America. That proved to be impossible. Today, he is settled comfortably as a professor of economics at the University of New Mexico. Writing on the twentieth anniversary of the Hungarian Revolt, he posed some poignant questions for his once bold freedom-fighters. At the same time he defined unwittingly the spiritual dilemma of so many people in our congregations: unprecedentedly free to pursue the good life, tragically un-free to be possessed by genuine goodness.

> We have freedom and material rewards, but are we really happy in this joyless society? . . . Do we have real friends with whom we can sit down for a conversation about personal things, music, literature, politics, legends? Are we still able, after the second bottle of wine, to cry with laughter and laugh with tears? Doesn't the lack of strong and emotional relationships drive us, along with our American acquaintances, into the arms of a predatory psychiatrist? . . . And we, old revolutionaries, are not the same as we were. Our generous leisure time, created by the labor-saving devices of a technologically advanced society, is used up while we are glued to the TV watching our favorite football team.[11]

There is enough truth in what Jonas says about middle-class Americans who make up the mainline Protestant, Roman Catholic, and Orthodox churches—and provide the majority of their clergy—to sober every preacher who enters an American pulpit. Tens of millions of Americans who cannot afford Europe, Hawaii, or Acapulco to escape boredom go instead to Las Vegas or Atlantic City. Millions more who cannot afford Las Vegas or Atlantic City patronize state-sponsored lotteries, big-time bingo, bet on the ponies, join a sports pool, or buy mutual stocks—hoping to strike it rich. Millions of others who do not gamble with their dollars, gamble with their family relationships, jobs, and personal lives—with alcohol, heroin, high speeds on the highway, sex for kicks—all in a vain effort to escape boredom. And millions more, grown grim in their pursuit of happiness, don't give a damn anymore. Bent on pursuing loneliness, they are persuaded that "life is a cheap bottle of wine." They do not seem to know where the good wine is stored—or care anymore. For them, the party is over.[12]

These are many of the people to whom we preach. Some are more successful in business and the professions, politics and the entertainment industry than others, but most of these, too, are existing without meaning, earning their livelihood from work in which they see little purpose, facing tomorrow without a lively hope that life can be authentic. Josephine Hendin, professor of contemporary literature at the New School for Social Research, in a stimulating, controversial study of American fiction since 1945, also identifies this emptiness in the novels of post World War II, titling her book, *Vulnerable People*.[13] Accidie—psychic paralysis—is a dominant theme in contemporary literature because it is a reality in contemporary life. It seems to be endemic to our culture. For serious ministers to live and preach in this cultural climate is to experience anguish, for if our "church" members are bereft and lost, and many are, it is in part because we preachers, bereft and lost ourselves, have failed both Christ and them by our half-hearted preaching which stems from our casual commitment to God.

Professor Jonas, concluding his article on the Hungarian Revolt, wrote, "No one asks for our story anymore, no one knows why we arrived here, and there are moments when we do not know either." [14] If the story of Jesus and his love is not getting into the congregations of America today, it is not only because our people do not ask for it, but also because we preachers, too much in love with this present world, remember it poorly, prepare it carelessly, and tell it half-heartedly. No preacher can proclaim the Word persuasively unless he or she knows God's story in depth and experiences first-hand the love that will not let go.[15] That is *what* we are called to preach. That is *why* we preach.

In the next three chapters, we shall examine explicitly the preacher's need to grow in grace as a Christian person and in vocational competence as a minister of Christ, and, implicitly, the congregation's need to grow in these areas also.

4 The Preacher's—and the Congregation's— Need to Grow

Forgetting what is behind me, and reaching out for that which lies ahead, I press toward the goal to win the prize which is God's call to the life above, in Christ Jesus.
— Philippians 3:13-14 (NEB)

HE LATE R. E. C. BROWNE, for many years the rector of St. Chrysostom's, Manchester, England, made this seasoned observation about preaching: "A minister of the Word who writes about preaching writes as a learner to other learners, and, like them, he is haunted by the sermon that no one is great enough to preach." [1] A century earlier, Henry Ward Beecher advised the divinity students at Yale: "It will take years and years before you are expert preachers. . . . You are getting ready to study when you begin to preach." [2] In 1946, James S. Stewart, in his Warrack Lectures on Preaching at Edinburgh University, declared: "When you have been preaching for twenty years, you will be beginning to realize how incalculably much there is to learn. ." [3] Biblical preachers are learners to the end of their days.

Christ is the same yesterday, today, and forever. But everything and everyone else changes, including human perceptions of God.[4] Those clergy who immerse themselves in biblical tradition get a sound perspective on change and growth as well as on sin and liberation and contemporary social and political issues. They discover that it has always been hard to sing the Lord's song in an alien land. But the difficulties in singing the Lord's song in today's alien culture are substantial. "Contemporary Christian preachers find themselves in a crossfire of conflicting tensions. Culturally, on the one hand, they are distant from the early Christians and much of the New Testament terminology, but at home in modern society. By faith, on the other hand, the preacher is one with the apostolic belief but hostile to the diminished existence imposed by secular humanism. And so, he faces a stiff challenge."[5]

This anguished learning process is part of the growing edge where effective biblical preachers and servant congregations work and wait, exult and despair, speak out and keep silent, venture boldly for Christ and hide behind dead traditions. Yet keeping alert to their need to grow, both realize slowly that they are growing in their ability to discern God's Word and that they are discovering firsthand that Christ is the power that transforms persons and sets these new creatures to work telling the Christian story abroad and building a just society for the sake of God's kingdom.

Most preachers stumble into competence occasionally because the gospel's riches are inexhaustible and the Spirit of the Lord is powerful. But they soon discover that it is difficult to preach a good sermon that does any good, and, having done it once, to do it again and again and yet again. Biblical preaching demands vocational skills. Even more, it requires that the preacher become a new creature in Christ. We fail more often than we succeed in climbing out of our cultural cocoons to think God's thoughts after him. We stumble more than we stride in following Christ. On a particular Sunday, we preach a sermon that is gloriously lucid in setting Christ before our people only to cloud his countenance in the sermon on the following Sunday. Colin Morris, after two decades of preaching in South Africa and England, declared: "Biblical preaching is not difficult; it is strictly impossible." [6] He means, of course, as every preacher knows from experience, that our best efforts under God's Spirit only *reflect* his mystery and glory, righteousness and grace. But those reflections in Christ-centered sermons provide more than enough light to lead people through an otherwise impenetrable darkness.

We preachers must grow as Christian persons and as effective ministers of Christ. If a revival of biblical preaching is to occur in our time, we must let go of our yen for center stage and dedicate our daily work to God, learn to handle personal criticism and rejection for the sake of the gospel, and concentrate first on the majesty and goodness of God rather than on the magnitude of social and ecclesiastical problems. It is the light of the gospel that illuminates these problems and equips us to address them effectively. It is the power of the gospel that keeps us in battles that often go against our hope for justice and love—here and now. Convinced through firsthand encounters that Christ is Lord, supported and corrected by the biblical tradition and the faith of the church, we preachers must learn to love the world enough "to defy it again, exasperate it, make its smug complacencies miserable, sting its calloused spirit alive. . . . The most subversive of all our hope . . . is the almost irresistible tendency to fade completely into the general landscape . . . so that our voice sounds precisely like the voice

of the man in the street and the methods we proclaim are
the methods he fashions." [7]

We must let the gospel keep alive this tension between
the church and the world, and between God's will and
our own. We, and our people, need desperately to grow
up in Christ. We need to go into our churches regularly
to worship God in beauty and truth and to learn his ways.
We need to go daily to a closet prayer room to petition
for ourselves, our people, and the world that ignores us
and in some quarters hates us. We need to stake out a
quiet place to study and reflect on God's Word—and then
do God's truth in our homes, the marketplace, the political arena, and preach and teach it to our people. We need
to recast our secular values in the light of Jesus' Sermon
on the Mount. In a world torn apart by human power, it
is crucial that we grow in our commitment to Christ's kind
of power (Mark 10:42-45). Jurgen Moltmann put this
elemental need succinctly:

> True dominion does not consist of enslaving others
> but in becoming a servant of others; not in the exercise
> of power, but in the exercise of love; not in being served
> by, but in freely serving; not in sacrificing the subju-
> gated but in self-sacrifice.[8]

This will require tremendous Christian growth (disciplined response to God's Word) on the part of ministers
and laity alike. Preachers, like their contemporaries, travel
the same broad highways that lead to personal frustration
and social chaos. But biblical preachers are no longer lost;
Christ has found them. They are in other hands than their
own. When they stray, they know the way home and take
it penitently and gladly. In Christian experience, the
opposite of sin is faith, not righteousness. The preacher is
not the Way; he points to the Way and helps others to

see it from his first-hand knowledge. "The necessity of preaching resides in the fact that when God saves a man through Christ he insists on a living, personal encounter with him here and now in the sphere of present personal relationships." [9] There are no draftees, conscripts, or mercenaries in Christ's corps of messengers—only willing co-workers.

Finally, God's messengers struggle to accept the fact of their preaching. Unlike the pulpiteer who "has an itch only an audience can scratch," God's heralds go forth reluctantly, experiencing anguish as well as joy in carrying on the preaching function of Christ's ministry. They learn early in their ministry that those who reject the Word often reject its bearer. That can be devastating. Preachers, like other human beings, want to be accepted, appreciated, loved. Jeremiah complained bitterly to God that his people had rejected him (Jer. 2:8). Paul, wrestling with the rejection of his person, wrote, "It is a small thing that I be judged of men." One need not be a student of Freud to recognize that the Apostle cared intensely about being accepted. Jesus cared, too. Touched by all our human frailties, he asked his disciples poignantly, "Will you also go away?" (Luke 22:19). To be rejected or deserted is a searing experience. Faced with that threat, many preachers surrender their convictions rather than risk the pain of personal rejection and isolation. Servants of the Word, tempted daily to deny their Master, cry out more often than their families or congregations or colleagues ever know: "It is too much that I should be called to preach the gospel in its offense and healing; deliver me from the agony of it."

Authentic preachers do not covet the preaching office, never become wholly comfortable in it, try at times to escape it, yet work at it diligently because the love of

Christ constrains them to it and sustains them in it. Karl Barth defined this ambivalence: "Preaching is an act of daring, and only the man who would rather not preach and cannot escape from it ought to ever attempt it." [10] Luther confessed from the pulpit now and again that he would escape preaching if he could. When he was studying for the Order of St. Augustine, he complained to his spiritual father, Staupitz, that preaching would kill him. Toward the close of his ministry he was still complaining that the office of preaching was a burden. Harry Emerson Fosdick confessed at the end of his ministry that preaching had never been easy for him and preaching "at the start was often exceedingly painful." Martin Luther King, Jr. preached under divine constraint. The world—and too often the church—does not understand that these inner-directed preachers cannot be bought off, compromised, or intimidated. King's letter from a Birmingham jail to the eight church leaders who had urged him to slow down the Black protest movement, places him in the direct line of Jeremiah and Peter. The origin of biblical preaching is in God's Word. The authority for a particular person preaching it is God's direct call (Gal. 1:11-2:21).

So, let the fumblers and the bumblers among us, the slow-witted and the recalcitrant, the weak and the proud —all of us—take heart: biblical preaching is not reserved for an intellectual, moral, or spiritual elite who choose to preach as a favor to God. He chooses, calls, enables, and undergirds us ("Stand up, mortal man. . . ."—Ezekiel) to be his ambassadors, deputies, heralds. Paul was not professionally skillful as a preacher if we can trust his self-evaluation: "I was with you in weakness, and in fear, and in much trembling" (1 Cor. 2:3 and 2 Cor. 10:10). That is not a description of the sophisticated style of a John Fitz-

gerald Kennedy or the self-assured manner of a Franklin
Delano Roosevelt or the olympian presence of a Winston
Spencer Churchill. It is, however, a fair description of
all earnest preachers ascending the pulpit stairs to preach
—and facing thereafter the task of preparing another sermon. "In weakness, and in fear, and in much trembling,"
is the gnawing condition of preachers who understand the
enormity of their task.

But Paul had more to say about his preaching. "My . . .
preaching was not with enticing words of man's wisdom,
but in demonstration of the Spirit of power" (1 Cor. 2:4).
In spite of his "unprofessionalism," Paul's preaching was
effective because he preached the Word. He admitted
readily that the vessel was not pure gold so as to point
out more clearly that the treasure made the difference.
So you and I—loving Christ, immersed in the scriptural
witness to God's self-revelation in history, possessed of
average emotional resilience and intellectual curiosity,
and having in hand a carefully prepared sermon—ascend
the pulpit stairs week after week, guided and heartened
by Paul's and Luther's and King's experience before us,
and our own, that God does not withhold his Spirit and
power from our preaching. Wherever clergy are alert, responsive, and faithful to the Word, many people know
from the content of their preaching, their devotion to
Christ, and their compassion for underloved people that
the kingdom of God is at hand.

But people do turn away from God's Word in preaching. To grow as a Christian minister is to accept this
truth as an inevitable response of some to the gospel. The
American church, in bondage to a success-oriented culture, must face up to this dark side of biblical ministry.
It must learn again that the early church, born under the
cross, was nailed to it daily. Human freedom makes faith

problematical. Because God respects every person's free-
dom it is, as Kierkegaard observed, "dreadful freedom."
Everyone is free to choose life or death (Deut. 30:19). On
Calvary, Jesus saved one thief while the other was lost.
The Rich Young Ruler turned his back on Jesus. The
Prodigal's brother sulked in the shadows outside the
homecoming party. Judas hanged himself. A few, like
Adolf Hitler, go to demonic length to extinguish the Light.
The holocaust that annihilated six million Jews, our own
nation's scorched earth policy in Vietnam and its "incur-
sion" (invasion) into Cambodia, Mao's massacre of millions of Chinese, the Soviet's death camps and expulsion
of Solzhenitsyn, and the Cambodian "purification" in
which hundreds of thousands have been killed by their
leaders demonstrate that people in our day deny and defy
God as readily as they did in Jesus' generation. Neither
transcendental meditation, nor training in self-assertive-
ness, nor possibility thinking, nor career-oriented clergy
can free people from pride and selfishness, cowardice and
despair. Only the proclamation of the cross can do that.

Inevitably, those clergy and lay leaders who accept
God's strategy for preaching his Word encounter stub-
born resistance in secular American communities, pious
congregations, and management-oriented denominations.
This resistance to God's truth among decent church people has multiple roots in our culture. But the taproot of
every person's resistance to God's Word in preaching in
our day is precisely what it was in the first century: a
human ego that exalts itself above God. Some people like
living in the far country; they prefer life there to facing
themselves honestly as the Prodigal did. They turn aside
God's call to repentance, avoid self-discipline, cringe at
the mention of sacrificial service. They do not want to
give Christ his rightful place above ego, family, church,

and nation. In the church itself many members want only a casual relationship with Christ. But the Lord will have none of that: "No man can serve two masters. . . ." People the world over, in all generations, seek to escape cross-bearing as single-mindedly as our colonial ancestors fled smallpox epidemics in their day.

Every minister who has ever engaged in the concrete, specific preaching of the demands and promises of God discovers that such preaching creates tension, stirs controversy, incites conflict. In our culture, it is convenient for the church to forget that Jesus predicted controversy and conflict wherever God's Word is preached. It is the genius of biblical preaching to expose human piety, the religion of nationalism, cherished secular values and goals, the religion of civility, social myths (for example, *all* blacks/Jews/women/Hispanics/Wasps are . . .), manipulative methods employed by church and state, and human perversity as enemies of God.[11] When this exposure is accomplished in the congregation, denomination, and community, some people are infuriated; others are indifferent; a few are set to hard thinking. Dialog between pulpit and pew becomes dialog between the church (its members) and the world. This dialog cannot be contrived. It is the fruit of biblical preaching and evangelical teaching. "The truth of the Gospel," Browne reminds us, "cannot be expressed in set formulae but only in authentic forms which are characteristic of the style of the preacher—and the style of the preacher must be characteristic of the man (woman)." [12]

When a church is empty—if the community is not sinfully over-churched or the congregation stripped of its spiritual vitality by a band of die-hards who want their own way rather than God's will—the pulpit is empty. Paul Althaus observed: "People are not tired of preaching; they are tired of our preaching." Parish pastors must live with that judgment, some knowing that it is true most of the time and others knowing that it is true some of the time. The tragedy is that most ministers *could* be responsible biblical preachers if they were willing to grow as Christian persons and work diligently at their vocations. God does not forsake those who give themselves in disciplined obedience to his Word.

Biblical preaching is remembrance and report; it is an event rooted in history. It is also interpretation of and personal testimony to Christ; it is Christ appealing by a particular preacher. Authentic Christian preachers demonstrate that the God of Abraham and Moses, Jeremiah and Hosea, Paul and John Wesley, Simon Peter and James Stewart is at work in their preaching because he is at work in their persons.

> The best sermons come from men and women whose wholesome personality, vigorous personhood, alert mind, and Christian consecration are gathered up in a power to communicate, based less on cleverness or strategy than on achievement of being. It is the total person who is the bearer of the gospel. . . .[13]

We turn next to consider how the biblical preacher grows in vocational competence and Christian personhood, and how his or her growth interacts with the congregation's growth.

5 On Preparing to Prepare the Sermon — Part I

Fill your minds with those things that are good and that deserve praise; things that are true, noble, right, pure, lovely, and honorable.
—Philippians 4:8 (GNB)

SERMON PREPARATION OCCURS ON TWO LEVELS of experience. The first is long-range: the daily study of the Scriptures, systematic reading in theology, disciplined reading in many fields of knowledge, and theological reflection on all three. It also rests on the preacher's first-hand experience in relating to persons in his or her marriage and family; to parishioners in sickness and death, vocational crises, teaching, day-by-day living, and administration of the parish; to fellow-citizens in one's community and nation, *and* on one's maturing relationship with Christ. All this is done without deliberate thought about sermon-making. Grist for the mill, it produces chaff and grain. It is preparing to prepare the sermon. It is part of the preacher's lifetime work and service.

The other level in preparing sermons is the conscious, disciplined work required to make a particular sermon. It has to do with the reading, studying, reflecting, praying, writing, pruning, and rewriting that go into the prepilation of the sermon for the following Sunday or for a series of sermons scheduled for a later date. We shall consider the first level of preparing to prepare the sermon in this chapter and the next. The second level, sermon-making and the act of preaching, will be addressed in chapters 7 through 10.

Each preacher discovers how to become open to the promptings of God's Spirit. Each has his or her own ways of developing a well-trained mind and a compassionate heart. Each comes into his or her own preaching style. But all preachers are alike in this. They need source materials for sermons. They need cultural breadth to preach the Word in depth. They need to learn how to prepare sermons competently without diminishing the time required for doing other essential functions of ministry and without neglecting their families. They need to learn self-discipline. They need inspiration in the study as well as in the pulpit, sick room, counseling chamber, and classroom. They need to pray not only before preparing and preaching the sermon but also while they are preparing to prepare it.

Content preaching is within the reach of every serious pastor. An insatiable desire to learn, consistent and persistent hard work, and the courage to be wounded—more than stunning talent—divide effective preachers from ineffective ones. The primary need of every preacher, as of every Christian, is the quickening of the human spirit by God's Spirit. That is pure gift. It cannot be commanded, coerced, or contrived. The wind blows where it will, and the Spirit of God moves according to his purposes. But as the week-end sailor sets his sail to catch the wind, so preachers and lay people learn to be open to the Spirit's sudden coming in personal meditation, in prayer and reflection, in service to others, and in the midst of daily work. There is a certain anti-intellectual cast of mind in some quarters of the church that looks upon serious study as a barrier to the Spirit. These people, lay and clergy, despise what they are too indolent to practice.

We can develop personal disciplines that heighten our awareness of and broaden our sensitivity to the Spirit's promptings. We can train ourselves to expect the unexpected. We may not find "sermons in stones" as Shakespeare suggested, but the discerning eye and the sensitive ear will alert us to the leadings of the Holy Spirit whose gifts are plentiful. Tragically, the Spirit's work and person are, in effect, ignored in the church today. "We have lost our nerve and our sense of direction and have turned the divine initiative into a human enterprise." [1] The Third Person of the Trinity was a presence in the apostles' preaching and teaching and in Paul's theology, preaching, and letterwriting. God's Spirit is as active in the twentieth century as he was in the first century, but to be open to his promptings requires study, reflection, hard thinking, prayer, and daily work. Apart from the Spirit's work, preaching is not biblical.

We shall speak first about books. Serious reading brings another human being's mind and spirit, perceptions and judgments, convictions and prejudices into direct contact with our minds and spirits, challenging our perceptions and convictions. Unless there is serious dialog between the reader and the author, the reader's imaginative faculties are not stirred. Careless reading and slipshod study are not productive. It is tragic that so many preachers do not wrestle with ideas and concepts and words in the service of God's Word—are not systematic, thoughtful readers of serious works in theology, cultural history, literature, biography, philosophy, sociology, psychology, and the sciences. Some sermons are thin because they are carelessly prepared: a stream of ideas looking for a structure. Others are thin because the preacher has little of substance to share: a stream of sentences looking for an idea. Both kinds of sermons, full of sound—and sometimes a fury born of the preacher's own frustration—are an insult to God, an offense to thoughtful parishioners, and a self-enacted crime against the preacher's calling.

The first book that calls the preacher to disciplined study from seminary days until death or mental disability is the Bible. Some people say that the Bible is the most widely distributed book and the least read. That is only partially true. It is the most widely distributed book; it is not the least read. Millions of people in the churches use the Bible devotionally every day. Tens of thousands of people—bruised and bleeding from their unequal bouts in a competitive, uncaring society—flip through its pages in hotel and motel rooms from Bar Harbor to Acapulco, London to Hong Kong, Tokyo to Capetown. It is read by thousands of people in every hospital in the "Christian" world. It is studied chapter by chapter and verse by verse in thousands of small Bible study groups in churches, homes, industrial plants, and places of business.

The Bible is used more widely than any other "book" in print in Europe and North America. The late Boris Pasternak, Russian poet and celebrated author of *Doctor Zhivago*, thought of "the Bible as being mainly an inexhaustible source of creative inspiration, as the starting point for an infinite number of ideas in literature and art: 'The Bible is not so much a settled text as a notebook for the whole of mankind.'" [2] E. B. White, the celebrated American essayist and writer of children's stories that are literary works of art, traveled across America in a Model T Ford when he was young (1922). On the left running-board of his Ford was a book box "within easy reach of the driver so that he may lean over and bring up the Holy Bible or Putnam's Word Book without slackening his pace." [3] Abraham Lincoln's spirit was shaped by God's Word, and his style bore the marks of the King James Bible. The young Albert Schweitzer, already an able professor of theology and a gifted organist, read the New Testament story of Dives and Lazarus, brooded over it, and was motivated to go to medical school and then to Africa to serve the underloved. Jesus entered the synagogue, opened the scroll of Isaiah, and began to read. Again and again in his brief, intense ministry, Jesus prefaced his teaching, "It is written. . . ." From the wilderness to Calvary, Jesus fortified his tempted human ego with his Father's Word. His anguished human cry, "My God, why have you forsaken me?" resonates from the twenty-second Psalm.

Nonetheless, a substantial portion of mainline Protestant clergy admit that they do not *study* the Scriptures systematically after graduating from seminary. By study, one means an uninterrupted hour or two every day spent digging critically into a book at a time, a biblical concept, a biblical personality, the prophetic tradition in the Old Testament, the development of worship in the Old and New Testaments, the conflicting accounts of human beings' relationship with the natural world—and so much more. A lifetime of study barely scratches the surface of the Bible's truth about God, human beings, and how they get together in Christ to the Father's satisfaction and the children's liberation. The focus of biblical preaching then is always Christ in whom God and mortals come face-to-face. Luther observed, "We preach always Him, the true God and Man. This may seem a limited and monotonous subject, likely to be soon exhausted, but we are never at the end of it." An hour a day, certainly two when that is possible, given to Bible study provides the best preparation for biblical preaching, along with the preacher's steadfast devotional use of the Scriptures. Preachers who study the Scriptures in depth discover riches they cannot exhaust in a lifetime of preaching. They will not hunt for texts or passages for exposition; these will find them in God's own time. God's first word to us, as to Augustine, is, "Take and read."

Disciplined study, prayer for guidance, and sustained reflection open us to God's truth in the Scriptures and in daily living. Freud, Jung, and Frankl have enlarged our awareness of the workings of the unconscious mind. Skinner has demonstrated how the human will is amenable to external direction and control. A constellation of able historians has broadened our knowledge of yesterday's events and their meanings in American and world history. A brilliant array of scientists have demonstrated our capacity to discern order and meaning in the natural world. We desperately need God's Word to make sense from all this. Back of the known self is the unknown self and other unknown selves. Back of the known universe is the unknown universe. We do not find God; he is not lost. We are lost; God finds us. Life is revelation as well as discovery. "From Incarnation to culture is a straight line, for the determination of God to embody his ultimate Word places man's relation to that Word inextricably in the web of historical circumstances. The Word is not naked; it is historically embodied." [4] We must know God as he reveals himself in Christ and, at the same time, understand our culture if we are to preach biblically.

Preachers who study the Scriptures systematically discern and experience the living Word in the Spirit-prompted human language of the Bible. Any suggestion that this does not happen in spite of different doctrines of inspiration among clergy and laity would be to make of historical criticism, or equally of the doctrine of verbal inspiration, an authority above Scripture itself. God's activity is larger than anyone's view of the Scriptures. I am not implying, however, that solid historical criticism—used intelligently in tandem with one's understanding of the relationship between revelation and history—is not the more excellent way. Employed responsibly, it sharpens the committed Christian's ability to discern God's Word in the Bible (Chapter 2).

Biblical preaching is done by clergy who live with immediacy in the world of the Bible, who immerse themselves in the Scriptures daily, who open their whole person to the Lord of the Scriptures and wait patiently yet expectantly for God's Word to them, and who then proclaim it in their historical situations as Amos and Micah did in theirs. Gardner Taylor, speaking from thirty years in the parish ministry, reminds us that God's Word in human language is heard, seen, and spoken:

> Altogether too much preaching, particularly in what are called the mainline churches, is too flat, too horizontal, too colorless, too unimaginative. Much of this can be overcome if those who preach would catch the sounds and sights and smells of the accounts recorded in the Bible. Enter as much as you can into the climate of each scene. Let the imagination and the mind work at the same time. Hear in the words of biblical record, the long, solemn, and yet tender love call of the Everlasting God aimed at His erring and straying creation.[5]

The Bible is indispensable for biblical preaching. *That* truth needs to be engraved on the mind and heart of every man and woman ordained by the church.

Other reading should be directed to broadening and

deepening the preacher's factual knowledge and understanding of American history in particular and the history of civilization in general. A broad knowledge of the
history of ideas, issues, personalities, and of wise and
unwise human decisions is crucial to effective biblical
preaching. The preacher should also read a scholarly book
or two on the Russian Revolution, the Soviet Union under
Stalin, and the People's Republic of China; and on India,
Japan, Latin America, and several of the emerging Afri-
can nations. If Amos spoke for God against the rich who
oppressed the poor in eighth-century Israel, today's authentic preachers will surely have a Word from the Lord
against powerful persons who exploit the poor in this nation and throughout the world, multi-national conglomerates that place profits above people, and rich nations that
callously allow thousands of human beings to starve every
day while they build "new barns" for their wealth.

Too much current preaching is unfocused, general
rather than specific, because so many clergy lack an
in-depth knowledge of world and American history. They
have little appreciation of the regional, cultural, and ethnic differences which divide us as a people in these United
States.[6] There are a score of reasons why American clergy
have taken extreme positions on social-political issues, or,
more often, no position at all. But a primary reason is that
so few know the history of this nation—its past and present internal and external relationships. Every theological
school should offer or require as a prerequisite a good
course in American political-social-economic history, an
equally solid survey on the "third" and "fourth" worlds,
an overview of the history of minorities in the United
States, and a history of ideas in Western thought, 1600-
1950. "The great object, in trying to understand history,"

Lord Acton wrote in 1880, "is to get behind men and to grasp ideas." [7]

These courses would open seminarians to some appreciation of the regional, class, and racial conflicts in America and the crucial interaction of more and more human beings and political states in the world. Technological man is "on a course which could alter dangerously and perhaps irreversibly the natural systems of his planet upon which his biological survival depends." [8] Courses in contemporary theology based on English and American literature and a semester on American fiction since 1945 would be helpful to seminarians, too, especially in their preaching and pastoral counseling.

The preacher should become well acquainted with English and American literature and some of the enduring works in nineteenth and twentieth-century French and Russian literature. One would judge that a minister with a baccalaureate degree from a four-year liberal arts college and a divinity degree from a three or four-year accredited theological school would have read Melville, Howells, Dreiser, Fitzgerald, Hemingway, Faulkner, Dickens, Thackeray, the Bronte sisters, Graham Greene, and Evelyn Waugh; Balzac, Hugo, Proust, and Camus; Tolstoy, Dostoevsky, and Solzhenitsyn before he or she was thirty. That is not the case. Only a minority of clergy have read widely in the literature of the West. Fewer still are conversant with English poetry from Donne and Coleridge to W. H. Auden and Stephen Spender, or with American poetry from Walt Whitman to Robert Frost and Sylvia Plath. Scarcely any know Shakespeare beyond "out damned spot" and "to be or not to be." Few expose their spirits to art and music.

Thomas Jefferson, the first-rank intellectual among American presidents, encouraged his friends to read good

novels. "Everything," he declared, "is useful which con-
tributes to fix the principles and practices of virtue." [9]
People are influenced to constructive action by reading
novels that reveal human nature (Herman Melville's
Moby Dick), middle- and upper-class social mores (John
O'Hara's *From the Terrace*), and racial prejudice (Laura
Z. Hobson's *Gentlemen's Agreement* and Harper Lee's
To Kill a Mockingbird). One of the most striking examples
of a novel's influence in American history is Harriet
Beecher Stowe's portrayal of slavery in her popular book,
Uncle Tom's Cabin. That book did for the Union in 1860
what Pearl Harbor did for the United States in 1941!
Michael Harrington's, *The Other America,* had a signifi-
cant impact on the American mind in the early 1960s.

Preachers should also read recent American fiction.
Even if it is what many critics say it is, "merely a record
of spiritual and emotional impoverishment"—and I agree
that much of it is—we preachers will get deeper insights
into this poverty among our parishioners by reading this
fiction. In American fiction since 1945 there is also a facet
of the recent American experience: what is happening to
middle-class people in a technological society; how desperately many of them pursue meaning and freedom in
affluence, power, sex, drugs; and how jaded, turned off,
many people are. The holistic and anarchic fiction written
since World War II

> may be seen as a protest against the human condition
> both for its finality, thanks to death, and its rigidity,
> thanks to convention. Although our novels are not, in
> the main, novels of ideas, they are concerned in simple,
> concrete ways with contesting the origins and ends of
> human activity. . . . In our middle-class mainstream fic-
> tion, our spiritual condition is imprinted in a revolution
> of sensibility, boring into questions of character, mean-
> ing, and significance.[10]

American fiction since World War II—from Wouk's *The Caine Mutiny* and Jones' *From Here to Eternity* to Haley's *Roots* and Lessing's *Summer Before the Dark*—poignantly presents men and women, white and black, struggling with personal crises and possible solutions in a dehumanized society. The gospel is pure gift to desperately searching, lost people. They deserve to hear it.

Of course, the alert preacher also reads novels to be exposed to the high uses of language—how expert writers describe the commonplace events of life. Robert Penn Warren, John Updike, Doris Lessing, and Saul Bellow are masters of prose-writing. Any preacher's style will improve from reading them and other literate novelists carefully, and literate nonfiction writers like Galbraith and Eisley and Barzun. Imaginative writers like J. R. R. Tolkein and C. S. Lewis and poets like Keats and Eliot and Frost are splendid teachers too.

Serious, reflective reading is an imaginative encounter with a particular author's wisdom, insights, prejudices, convictions, and vision of life. The late Gilbert Highet, long-time professor of classical literature at Columbia University, caught this magnificently:

> . . . when I stand in a big library like the Library of Congress, or Butler at Columbia, or Widener at Harvard, or Firestone at Princeton, and gaze around me at the millions of books, I feel an earnest delight which is hard to convey except by a metaphor. These are not books, lumps of lifeless paper, but *minds* alive on the shelves. . . . one can call into range the voice of a man far distant in time and space and hear him speaking to us, mind to mind, heart to heart.[11]

Listen to John H. Snow responding to the challenge of Pierre Teilhard de Chardin's mind:

I heard about Teilhard in the late fifties when I was in a groping mood. I bought this book, *The Phenomenon of Man,* and tried to read it and felt about as uneducated as I have ever felt in my life. . . . A third of the way through it the vocabulary began to become familiar, and I could read it easily enough to get at its larger meaning. It is one of the few books I have ever read about which I can truly say that it changed my vision of the world. . . .[12]

Like others in my generation, I can echo Snow's experience from reading at the outset of my ministry two sets of Gifford Lectures, the first by William Temple and the second by Reinhold Niebuhr.[13] Those two men enlarged radically my Christian view of God, human beings, and the world. At the same time, Herbert H. Farmer gave me a theology for biblical preaching. And other authors have ushered me into larger worlds: Huizinga on the Middle Ages; Nietzsche on life without God; Dostoevsky and Berdyaev on human freedom; Melville on evil; Crane and Mailer on war; Jacob Burckhardt on culture; Bernanos on the possibilities of the parish; Eisley on the natural world; Compton and Weinberg on theoretical science; Jung and Allport on human nature; Luckman on the sociology of religion; Trevelyan, Macauley, Morrison, and Commager on English and American history; Barber on the presidential character; Arendt on revolution; Ward and Galbraith on economics—and scores more.

A word about newspapers. Instead of getting hooked on them, one should read selectively in several "national" papers *(New York Times, Washington Post, Christian Science Monitor)* and a European paper or two, especially, I think, the *Manchester Guardian* with its intellectual Marxist slant. The preacher must spend some time with the daily news, but anyone who spends much time on newspapers, even the best ones, is squandering precious time. One need invest only an afternoon in any major library with microfilm of the *New York Times* for 1966 or 1936 or 1906 to prove the validity of that observation. Newspaper reporting lacks perspective and depth; and investigative reporting, like psycho-history, must be read critically. In-depth articles in religious and secular magazines and journals are essential background reading for preachers who want to understand the culture in which they preach.

It is a life-style of sustained biblical study and wide cultural reading that helps the preacher to perceive the central truths about God and human beings in the Scriptures and, focusing clearly on both in the context of modern culture, to relate these truths in simple, direct, imaginative language in sermon after sermon. Millions of mainline Protestant and Roman Catholic lay people have never made a clear-headed, gallant commitment to Christ, because they have not heard him preached intelligibly. Biblical preaching is not possible if the preacher does not give at least two or three hours daily to hard study in biblical *and* secular sources. Ernest Fremont Tittle, persuasive preacher and social crusader in the 1930s and '40s, observed a generation ago:

> Too many preachers are lying down on the job. . . . The time which they do spend among their books, or to speak more accurately, in the same room with their books—what do they do with it? Mostly they kill it. . . .[14]

Times have changed radically since Tittle made that stinging criticism fifty years ago. Few preachers kill time in their studies anymore. They do not have studies! They have well-appointed offices where they counsel troubled parishioners, "administer" the parish, and convene committee meetings to discuss how to evangelize, how to do stewardship, and so on. If the pulpit is empty, it is because the preacher is empty, or the hearers want to be empty, or both. Without a study somewhere—a private place for reflection and meditation—the young preacher will become empty in a few years and the middle-aged minister will deteriorate into a caretaker, a manager, or a "professional" priest/pastor.

Too many clergy, pressed in theological discussions, turn one aside with the statement, "I'm a pastor, not a theologian." This false dichotomy thrives in the contemporary church. In some cases, the seminary failed with some of its graduates. In other cases, the church approved incompetents for ordination. In most cases, however, these clergy vegetated intellectually or their parishes domesticated them. All biblical preachers and evangelical teachers are well-seasoned theologians. Both functions of ministry require *theological* thinking. The problem here is biblical and theological as well as cultural. Clergy and lay people alike separate "love" from "truth" as readily as they separate preaching from the other functions of Christ's ministry. This reveals a severe fault in their understanding of biblical theology. Effective pastoral work cannot be done apart from biblical preaching which, in turn, rests on a sound biblical theology. The ordained minister is not the only theologian in the congregation, but he or she is appointed to be the chief theologian. It is a dereliction of duty to escape this responsibility of the office of ministry (Chapter 3).

The hoped for revival of biblical preaching, 1980-2010 —an era that will spawn unmatched technological, political, and social changes, some, perhaps, devastating—will require a large corps of preachers who are well-read. Critical judgment, enlarged and sharpened by sustained reading and serious communication with knowledgeable people in print, is required of all citizens in a Republic. It is a must for preachers who want to speak God's message effectively in this knowledge-laden, yet searching, unwise, confused, irrational, violent, lost world.

Preachers, perhaps the last of the generalists, bear a double burden of responsibility. On the one hand, they must be knowledgeable about their world. On the other hand, they dare not default on their responsibility to develop the vocational tool of theological reflection. It is precisely this skill of theological reflection, developed and honed in dialog with great theological and secular minds, that enables the preacher to engage in creative dialog with people in the world. One cannot read the Bible *by itself* and be an effective biblical preacher. Wide cultural reading is also essential. Somerset Maugham opined, "There is no more merit in having read a thousand books than in having ploughed a thousand fields." [15] That is true. Every honorable vocation contributes to a healthy, stable society. But ministers were not called to plow fields. We are called to preach God's Word responsibly. That cannot be done without serious, sustained study of the Bible and wide, disciplined reading in secular sources. All Christians are called to live with and by the Word in God's world.

6 On Preparing to Prepare the Sermon—Part II

We preach eternity; but when Jesus asks us, "Did you have enough of everything?" we will have to reply "Oh, no; we didn't have enough time." That is why we preach peace and radiate restlessness. . . . The faith is refuted by the incredibility of those who proclaim it.

—Helmut Thielicke

AT THIS POINT IN OUR DISCUSSION of preparing the sermon some will have cried out in frustration, "I don't have time to read much of anything in a demanding parish ministry." That is true. It is not easy for a pastor in a parish of four hundred persons or more to manage time for systematic study. I envy those English, Scottish, and American preachers who, from 1870 to 1950, could command the morning hours of every week day for uninterrupted reading and study. As late as 1946, James Stewart, still preaching at North Morningside Church in Edinburgh, could urge the hearers of his Warrack Lectures on Preaching to do precisely that.[1] Like most parish pastors, I must block out other times for reading and study—and do it. Each preacher "must order his life from the inside. . . . But order it he must."[2] If the preacher does not make time for reading critically and thinking reflectively—and the congregation tolerates superficial preaching—they will merely "play church" every Sunday for an hour or two. The book of Revelation conveys God's searing judgment on churches that are neither hot nor cold toward him. These congregations and their clergy, scarcely aware that God is alive and well and powerful, die a little every week.

There is another objection to systematic reading. How can the preacher, unless he or she lives near a large public library or a theological library, obtain good reading material? Most ministers are limited severely in their buying power, and the present cost of hardback editions is prohibitive. There are ways. Keep abreast of the paperback market; it is respectable and thriving. Major religious publishers offer original paperbacks and paperback reprints of solid biblical and theological works. Quality Paperbacks, Middletown, Pennsylvania, provides the better secular hardbacks in paperback editions within six months to a year of their original publication. Join several good book clubs; read the reviews; purchase four books a year. Share expenses with several colleagues and exchange books every three months or so. Announce to your congregation several times a year that you would be pleased to receive their used books, magazines, and journals. Keep alert for the annual book sales of publishers. Urgently ask your governing board for a generous annual book-journal-magazine-newspaper allowance. Review three or four books a year for the congregation on Sunday or weekday evenings. In cooperation with your committee on parish education, establish a parish library. Begin small and add only the best books and journals. Appoint a librarian and ask him or her to report monthly on new accessions. A good parish library is one of the pastor's resources, too.

Many books on preaching extol pastoral work as the best resource for sermon-making. That is not wholly true. First, information from counseling, hospital calls, home visitation, and evangelistic calls belongs in the preacher's head and heart—and private files—not in his Sunday sermon. Data received and gathered from human sources is privileged information. Cases do not belong in the pulpit, even with altered names or as composite cases. Parishioners are not "case studies" or source material for sermon illustrations. One can get that kind of material from broad reading in contemporary history and literature. The only case study that belongs in the pulpit is the preacher's own, and that rarely. Paul, an expert on this, is a proper model. He spoke often about his ministry and the spiritual condition of the congregations. But he spoke only occasionally about *his* conversion experience (1 Cor. 15:8-11 and Gal. 1:15ff.).

Since effective work in the pulpit is inseparable from effective pastoral work and responsible work in the community, preachers strike a balance between solitude and society, study and social involvements. A preacher who cannot because of emotional disability, or will not because of temperamental disability, relate in depth to people will not become a biblical preacher. No one can love God without loving his people. Today, many well-educated clergy construct solid sermons yet nothing happens when they preach because on the other six days of the week they do not risk the pain of relating openly to persons in their own families, parishes, and communities. Those preachers will preach ineffectively so long as they are isolated, unapproachable, rigid, arrogant, ill-at-ease, or arbitrary with people. These particular critiques, when they are true, testify to the preacher's insecurity as a person and to his or her underdeveloped love for people. Some clergy will need professional help to cope with their defensive, rigid personalities in the rugged give-and-take of a parish ministry oriented to the Word.

Most clergy, however, get free of their insecurities and self-consciousness and cautious loving as they become involved with the Word *and* the people God called them to serve. Learning to acknowledge and correct their own mistakes, they grow in personal security as well as vocational competence. Within a decade of parish ministry they discover a new dimension to their persons as a consequence of their deepening involvement with Christ and his people. They acknowledge gladly that one of God's best gifts is this new self—less preoccupied with ego demands, more emotionally secure, more compassionate, more resilient, more confident, more hopeful. "The experiences which illuminate the preacher's faith are not accidental happenings outside his responsible control; they are fruits of a style of life whose nature is largely hidden but which is active obedience to the Lord's injunction: 'He that loseth his life for my sake shall find it.' At the point where a man's individuality seems to be dissolving he becomes most individual and most powerful in the lives of others." [3] It is in *this* context that pastoral work is a resource for preaching.

Phillips Brooks, remembered as a mighty preacher of God's Word, preferred making pastoral calls to other functions of ministry. In a clergy meeting where preaching was being extolled and pastoral calling depreciated, Brooks interrupted to say, "I would like to do nothing but make pastoral calls and meet the people. Indeed, if I did not, I could not preach." [4] He was not talking about people as sources for sermon illustrations but about in-depth

Christian relationships as an essential resource for preaching. Living openly with others—family, parishioners, neighbors—is indispensable to biblical preaching. A person-to-person ministry keeps the clergy close to the people and the people close to their ministers. Harry Emerson Fosdick of Riverside Church kept in touch with persons through daily pastoral counseling. One of his most useful books, *On Being a Real Person*, came out of his pastoral counseling as well as his preaching ministry. Each fed the other. Faithful pastoral visitation and counseling and biblical preaching are inextricably bound together.

The biblical preacher, convinced that the parishioners do not define the *content* of sermons (God's Word) but need it desperately, is structured by the gospel to let people be hurt even as he or she accepts hurt in serving Christ responsibly. Preachers discover quickly that it is one thing to want to serve people with and from the Word and quite another to be willing to be made strong enough and wise enough and gentle enough to do it. Bonhoeffer had to learn that. Ten years later, Martin Luther King, Jr., a twenty-six-year-old Ph.D., pastor in Montgomery, Alabama, began to learn this obedience to Christ which also, in time, took him to a violent death. It is costly to follow Christ. Too many educated ministers and sophisticated lay people act as though Jesus could have avoided Calvary if he had exercised a little common sense, that sin is a word to be spoken rather than a human condition that requires Christ's cross to overmatch it.

When we emphasize that the biblical preacher loves people from Christ's own love, we are standing in the apostolic tradition (2 Cor. 6). When we take that stance, we too are enabled to love others—decent and treacherous, wise and foolish, generous and selfish—because God first loved us in our misery. Paul goes to the heart of it: "While we were yet in sin, Christ died for us." J. W. Stevenson, speaking of his early ministry in Scotland, put it this way: "But I was to learn also why . . . under one aspect, the church seems to be made up of men and women not better than the rest, and, under another set of circumstances, has the look of Heaven." [5] The pastor's love of his people is not a permissive, unrighteous love. It is a love, reflecting Christ's love, that truly cares for them as persons, encouraging them in a closer walk with Christ. Paul makes that clear: ". . . we have been approved by God to be entrusted with the Gospel, so we speak not to please men, but to please God who tests our hearts" (1 Thess. 2:3-4).

Like all shepherds, I have anguished over those who have dismissed Jesus' invitation whether from ignorance or willfulness or psychological disability. But for them, and us, the last word is a word of hope. When we cry out in some country far from home, "We don't have to live this degrading life; we can go home again," and do, the caring Father runs out to embrace us, his glad tears mingled with ours. What a rugged, demanding Word we preachers bear to others and ourselves, yet how gentle and life-resurrecting it is to those who come to their senses and, in their freedom, come home again! Biblical preaching is prophetic *and* pastoral. Either without the other is not biblical.

So the preparation of particular sermons begins months and years before they are preached. Looking back, the veteran preacher sees this clearly. As the farmer plows the field, sows the seed, cultivates the soil, and waits for God's harvest time, so too does the preacher, serving the same congregation through the years, prepare daily to prepare sermons that are preached a decade hence. And those sermons are the preacher's *own*. They come from his or her experience with God and people. In the late seventeenth century, Archbishop Fenelon of Cambrai in France spoke bluntly about the ineffective preacher of his day: ". . . some sermon books he has bought, and various collections he has made of purple patches wrested from their context and hit upon by good luck. . . . In a case like his, one cannot say anything strongly; one is certain of nothing; everything has a borrowed and patch-work look."⁶ Fenelon would be appalled by the "patch-work" sermons that some contemporary preachers offer their congregations. No minister can preach effectively what belongs to others or be confident in preaching what he or she has prepared haphazardly from a sermon book or two, a compilation of sermon illustrations, the local newspaper, and a last ditch prayer. God does not bless that kind of dishonest, slovenly work. Biblical preaching roots in the preacher's faith, biblical understanding, cultural breadth, pastoral work, and diligent, systematic preparation to prepare particular sermons.

In a serious discussion of preparing to prepare sermons, we must underscore the preacher's need for "the harvest of the quiet eye." Not only poets but scientists rely on it. But in our day the emphasis belongs on the word *quiet*. Parish clergy are culturally conditioned, as their parishioners and neighbors are, to be activists. "We have a live wire this time" is the inelegant way some lay leaders describe a promising new pastor. That view of ministry is unbiblical. It is also dangerous. Live wires that are improperly connected can be destructive! All too often, activist pastors, like Stephen Leacock's horseman, leap to the saddle and ride off in four directions at once. To be sure, all parish pastors have days when their ministry is "confusion roughly organized"; but some never get it together. They plan more than they pray, react more often than they act, speak before they have reflected carefully, and preach with little regard for content. Their pastoral work, too, is peripatetic. So, the biblical preacher prays daily for a quiet spirit. And the "harvest of the quiet eye" provides inexhaustible resources. Galileo's revolutionary concept of the universe, Faulkner's novels about Yoknapawtapha County, and Jesus' parables testify to that.

Some specific observations on preparing to prepare the sermon may be helpful.

First, you will need to take some notes. Do not overdo it. The human mind is not a computer, but it will handle more data and ideas than most of us ask of it. We train the eye, limb, and muscle in order to excel in football, baseball, tennis, golf, or swimming. The brain is not a muscle, but regular use strengthens its remarkable capacity. Read thoughtfully for a large grasp on truth and the enrichment of your own person. Do not read in search of sermon material. Let the material present itself. Require your mind to handle more and more material, year after year. Keep a simple, selective file.

Each preacher, of course, will find his or her own way. If you keep a sermon notebook and/or file cards, clean up both periodically. Until one learns to read critically and selectively he or she will collect and file ten useless items for every useful one. After three and a half decades in Christ's ministry, I have scarcely more than two thousand file cards (less than sixty a year) and no sermon notebooks. But I do outline the autumn and Lenten sermon series months in advance and keep several sermons working all the time. Over the years, I have trained a once indolent mind to retain much that I want to recall later. Anyone who works at this will be amazed at the capacity of the human mind to handle so much, so easily. This discipline also increases reading comprehension. But even with an extensive filing system, one cannot begin to acknowledge fully his or her debt to others. Be selective then in collecting and filing; work vigorously at absorbing the materials you read; reflect on them; use them in personal relationships. In future months and years, they will march unbidden into sermon after sermon because they are part of you.

Second, disciplined reading habits need not be compulsive. If one had nothing to do in this life except read, he or she could handle only a fraction of the published works and printed articles available today. Each of us needs guidance. It is available in competent review journals and secular book club publications. It is also available from competent contemporaries, especially lay people. If you are relating well to persons in your parish and community, and exciting their minds, they in turn will share creative resources with you. I am indebted to a host of parishioners and friends for consciousness-expanding books I would not have discovered myself.

It is the quality even more than the quantity of one's reading that enlarges his or her cultural understanding and sharpens one's perceptions. Five or six substantive books read reflectively each year will enrich the preacher more than fifty shallow books read hurriedly. Some books are worth reading more than once: H. Richard Niebuhr's *Christ and Culture,* for example. A few authors deserve to be our life-long companions: Tolstoy, Hugo, Melville, Dostoevsky, C. S. Lewis, William Temple, Milton, Shakespeare, Augustine. Of course, the Gospels and the Epistles, the Pentateuch and the Major Prophets, the Psalms, Daniel and Revelation, Jonah and Job, and the Minor Prophets deserve to be read hundreds of times in-depth.

The whole New Testament is barely the size of a single average-length contemporary novel!

Read for biblical and cultural understanding of God at work in his world and cosmos. Read for vocational competence. Read for critical knowledge. Read for personal fulfillment. Read to stimulate your imagination. Read, too, for relaxation. But never read mindlessly. Agatha Christie's mysteries deserve better than that! So do the spy stories of John LeCarre and Helen MacInnes. Get into dialog with Herodotus and Samuel Eliot Morrison; Plutarch and W. H. Auden; Solzhenitsyn and Shaw; T. S. Eliot and Sylvia Plath; Faulkner and Cheever; Joyce Carol Oates and Doris Lessing; Henry Fairlie and Daniel Schorr —and hundreds more. Everything one reads is grist for the theological mill. Reading is work, but it is privileged work. You can read as long as your faculties function; and then, one day in eternity you can turn these thousands of dialogs-in-the-mind into fascinating face-to-face encounters and eternal friendships.

Third, since a well-furnished mind, a sensitive spirit, and an active imagination require disciplined reading habits, the pastor may need to improve his or her reading skills. Many clergy have told me in conferences that they read slowly and/or comprehend poorly what they read. Usually, these handicaps go together. Both are correctable. Many people read slowly and comprehend unevenly because they do not view reading as work; they fail to get into serious dialog with the author. If you cannot teach yourself to read more rapidly and to comprehend more readily, take an accredited course in speed reading. Reading is a skill that preachers, like teachers, business executives, and Congress people, must possess to be effective in their work. Baron von Hugel opined that fifteen minutes of serious reading each day over a lifetime makes a substantial difference in one's cultural and spiritual outlook. And so it does. But biblical preaching over a lifetime requires much more than fifteen minutes of reading each day.

Fourth, the biblical preacher draws apart from the world daily to *reflect* on the Word, people in need of Christ, the siren calls of an alien culture, and the points in his or her own person where the world's enticing calls break through. To reflect means to consider, contemplate, concentrate, weigh, evaluate. It also means to throw back an image, mirror, shine, reproduce. As the Parthenon on the Acropolis reflects the glory that was Greece, as the Augustan Age reflects the grandeur that was Rome, as the American Constitution reflects the political philosophy of its framers, the biblical sermon reflects (mirrors) the mind that is in Christ Jesus. The products of the *reflective* mind are rich and far-reaching: Jesus in the wilderness reflecting on his mission; Augustine reflecting on the city of God and the decadent Roman Empire; Luther reflecting on Christ's saving work and the medieval church's meritorious concept of grace; Copernicus reflecting on the movement of the planets; Wesley reflecting on Luther's preface to the book of Romans; Descartes reflecting on the nature of being; Lincoln reflecting on the meaning of the Union; Bonhoeffer, in 1939, reflecting on his responsibilities to God and the German people; King reflecting on the plight of the Blacks and other oppressed minorities in America. . . . Reflection is hard work, but the harvest from it feeds those who hunger after life. It is indispensable to the preparation of biblical sermons.[7]

The enormous responsibility of doing biblical preaching sobers and humbles us. It need not paralyze us. It will not if we prepare to prepare. James Stewart's counsel is sound: "All your experience of God, all your acquaintance with life, all your knowledge of people, all your fellowship with the great minds of the centuries will come . . . to your aid." [8] So will the Holy Spirit as you pray and work over each sermon for fifteen or twenty hours every week.

> Many people have played themselves to death. Many people have eaten and drunk themselves to death. *Nobody has ever thought himself to death.* Thought is the only human activity which does not generate large quantities of harmful acids and alkalies. It is laziness, sloth, routings, stupidity, forcing their way in like wind through the shutters, seeping into the cellar like swamp water. [9]

One other facet of the preacher's private-social self needs to be examined. It is friendship. See to it, if you can and if they are willing, that your spouse and children are the friends of your mind as well as your heart. Pray God that these persons are your truest friends, and then work to make it so. Give before you expect to receive; understand before you seek to be understood; forgive before you ask to be forgiven; love as deeply as you want to be loved. Tragically, this is beyond some families. Charles Wesley's wife was a shrew; David's son, Absalom, was a murdering rebel; Phillips Brooks had no wife and family. But insofar as you are able, see to it that your spouse and children are the truest friends of your mind as well as your heart. The dialog in this privileged, intimate relationship enriches one's preaching because it enriches one's person.

Outside one's family, the preacher will have thousands of acquaintances, associates, admirers, and some enemies in the course of a lifetime dedicated to God's Word. In this circle, too, there are friendships that enrich and teach us, adversaries who correct us, enemies who catapult us into intercessory prayer. Surely, the preacher will count his or her parishioners as best friends. But, friends of the heart and mind, legion in heaven, are rare in this life. Apparently, Jesus had three men—Peter, James, and John —and three women—Mary, his mother, Mary Magdalene, and Mary of Bethany—whose company he especially delighted in.

C. S. Lewis avers that one's first life-long friend (outside one's family) is likely to be his or her alter ego, one "who first reveals to you that you are not alone in this world"; one who shares "your most secret delights." The second life-long friend, Lewis judges, is in a sense one's anti-self, even as the first is one's alter ego. "The second friend disagrees with you about everything. He shares your interests but approaches them all at a different angle. He has read all the right books but has got the wrong thing out of every one. . . . When you set out to correct his heresies, you find that he forsooth has decided to correct yours!" [10]

I have been privileged to have both kinds of friends for almost forty years. There is no way to calculate the debt my preaching owes to them because of what they have meant, and mean still, to me. Of course, there have been other friendships, hinted at in other chapters, which have profited my person and my preaching: men and women who taught me to appreciate literature and history; poetry, music, and art; politics and organization—and an indefatigable friend, Elton Trueblood, who kept at me to write until I did.

Friendships, true and real, are among God's most splendid gifts to human beings. Their contributions to one's learning to preach biblically are incalculable. There are no loners in the corps of God's effective preachers. Paul needed Timothy; Augustine needed the Bishop of Milan and Monica, his mother; Luther needed his beloved Katharine and his friend, Melanchthon. And, like them, we all need the Friend of our heart's and mind's desire, Christ.

Biblical preachers, in order to use their knowledge and personal experience in the service of God, must work to be theologians and, in fact, do theology their whole life through—to make everything subject to God's will in Christ. It is their theological perspective that brings unity to their biblical and secular studies, their pastoral work, their intimate friendships, and their weekly preaching. Biblical preachers make theological reflection an integral component in their life process, seeking to understand how and where biblical faith effects the transformation of human life and impacts on contemporary culture. The theologian interprets God's Good News. The preacher proclaims and teaches it. The pastor helps and heals persons from its inexhaustible resources. This is every parish minister's triple-pronged vocation: theology, preaching and teaching, pastoral care. It is the pastor's fidelity to God's Word that brings these functions together as Christ's ministry in the world. Lifelong preparation and study and prayer and pastoral work, under the authority of the Word, is the source of biblical preaching.

In the next chapter we shall inquire into the nature and purpose of the biblical sermon.

PART TWO

Preparing
and
Preaching
the Sermon

7 The Biblical Sermon: What Is It?

Gentlemen, this is a football.
—Vince Lombardi

A sermon is more like a concert than a coaching lesson.
—Theodore P. Ferris

The only thing in God's economy that can ever take the place of preaching is better preaching.
—Paul Scherer

IN THIS CHAPTER and in the next three chapters, we shall focus on sermon-making and the act of preaching. The proper place to begin is with fundamentals. What is the nature and purpose of the sermon?

When Vince Lombardi, an eminently successful professional football coach in the 1960s, was asked how he produced winning teams, he declared that any group of naturally-endowed football athletes could win more games than they lost if they concentrated on the fundamentals of the game—blocking, tackling, kicking, passing, pass-receiving, and running. After a close game won by his Green Bay Packers, Lombardi called a special session for Monday morning. Appearing before his players, he held a football above his head and announced: "Men, we need to review the fundamentals of the game. This is a football." Max McGee, so the story goes, drawled: "That's a little fast, coach. Go over that again." True or not, the story sets the stage for this chapter: to establish what a sermon is, define its basic purpose, and stress the importance of reviewing periodically the fundamentals of sermon-making.

The first step in getting at the fundamentals of sermon-making is to recognize clearly what a sermon is *not* and what it is *not* intended to be, and what, by its nature, it is *not* allowed to attempt. This negative analysis will allow us to focus more precisely on the true nature and purpose of the sermon. The sermon is *not* an essay, a public speech, a lecture, a sales pitch, or a solo performance. Ministers, learning how to preach effectively, check these basic distinctions as faithfully as pilots on a jet airliner review their detailed checklist before each takeoff. After three decades of preaching, I must still guard against preparing biblical-theological lectures. Unless my experienced associates keep alert, one is inclined to write insightful essays while the other tends to write critical social analyses.

The sermon is not an essay. An essay has a subject. A sermon has an object. An essay is written to be read privately.[1] A sermon is written to be proclaimed publicly. Both the essay and the sermon, well-done, awaken interest, communicate ideas, stir emotional responses. Each, serving its distinctive purpose, has its own form and style. But the object of the sermon, unlike that of the essay, is to communicate the unique message of God's good news to individuals so that they will decide for or against Jesus Christ.

The essay can communicate the writer's original ideas. That is not legitimate in a sermon if the preacher's "original" ideas are contrary to biblical truth. Emerson's celebrated essay on self-reliance propagates his personal values. It is a literary classic, but it is only a partial presentation of Christian truth. An essay can also describe any person the writer chooses for his subject. William Allen White's poignant essay, "Mary White," another classic, describes his memories of the person, character, and independent life-style of his beloved twelve-year-old daughter who was killed in a horseback riding accident. But a sermon that takes a person for its subject must demonstrate how that particular person was or is accepted by God, related or relates to Christ, served or serves persons as a Christ-figure so that the hearers decide for or against Christ. The aim of the essayist is the elucidation of a subject for the pleasure or edification of the reader. The aim of the biblical preacher is the presentation of God's good news for the transformation of responsive persons. The essay is written to be read. The biblical sermon is prepared to be proclaimed.

A sermon is not a public speech. It is spoken in a public place; the church is open to everyone. But a congregation assembled around the Word in preaching, teaching, sacraments, and Christian care is not a public audience. It is a gathering of the people of God, a colony of heaven, a little corner of God's kingdom. The sermon teaches biblical concepts (human nature, God's nature, faith) and seeks to relate the experience of persons with the living God. It aims to persuade people to examine biblical values and the view of history that has the cross at its center, and to act in the light of the gospel. It always testifies to the Christian God in one way or another. Unashamedly, it calls persons to accept Christ and enables them to do his commandments. "A sermon is a revelation of some aspect of the reality of God in reference to some human need or condition. . . . It is by nature a disclosure, an unveiling. . . ." [2] A sermon cannot do what an effective public speech will do—promote the speaker as well as his personal views. In effective biblical preaching, the medium is subordinate to the message; the earthen vessel is subservient to the treasure.

A sermon is not a biblical sermon if, deliberately or unwittingly, it promotes the preacher above God's message. Biblical preachers come to be highly valued in thousands of congregations throughout the world, not primarily for their personal gifts but because their persons and their preaching and pastoral work testify to the Living Word. They do not preach to impress people with their erudition but to inform, enlighten, and enable them from the resources of God's Word. Like other public callings, the parish ministry has built-in temptations to call attention to one's self. When that happens—and it does more often than it should—God's Word is obscured, its impact blunted, its appeal flattened. John the Baptist said of Jesus, "He takes rank before me" (John 1:15a, NEB). Jesus, called "good" by many, demurred, reminding his admirers that only God is good. An essential part of the biblical preacher's task is to get himself or herself out of the way in unveiling the mystery, majesty, and mercy of God, yet do it without denigrating the earthen vessel that bears the treasure. "The Christian preacher is not the successor of the Greek orator but of the Hebrew prophet. The orator comes with but an inspiration; the prophet comes with a revelation." [3]

A sermon is not a lecture. A lecture is designed to communicate information that is new (a physicist reporting new data to other physicists), professionally useful (a medical biologist teaching anatomy to first-year medical students), or interesting (a travel lecture). God's Word, new every morning, is dynamically useful to responsive persons. That is what the sermon communicates. In biblical preaching, emphases shift, accents change, forms and styles vary, but the basic content remains the same. Because biblical preaching is evangelical teaching and evangelical teaching is biblical preaching, I shall attempt here to delineate more sharply between the lecturer and the teacher.

The lecturer provides information as a cafeteria offers food; the listener selects what he wants and savors what he likes. The lecturer may be intellectually brilliant, but he or she rarely places demands on the whole person of the listener. Effective teaching, on the other hand, presents a body of truth that can be documented. But the presentation of it aims, beyond the validation of the material, is to motivate the student (hearer) to get involved with the material, to get at the meaning behind the facts. It seeks to awaken the hearer's desire to understand it fully and to apply it responsibly.[4]

Teaching is different in purpose, form, and style from lecturing. Teaching is a serious, open dialog between people. Lecturing is a performance (dull or exciting) by a person for persons and/or for sharing information with others. Gilbert Highet, Jacques Barzun, and Loren Eisley were university *teachers;* the classrooms of every college and university are crowded with *lecturers.*

If the distinction between teaching and lecturing is sharp, the difference between evangelical teaching and secular teaching is chasmic. Evangelical teaching communicates the gospel truth. Jesus came preaching (heralding, proclaiming) the good news that God was at hand to receive sinners. He also came teaching—forming the interior being of his hearers on the nature of God, human nature, the nature of faith, the need for repentance, the "giveness" of the new life in him, the responsibility of God's people to build up the Christian community, and their equal responsibility to work toward a just society for the sake of God's kingdom. Evangelical teaching is ethical instruction set in the power of the kerygma. If that power is lacking, moralistic teaching results.[5] Biblical preaching focuses on the kerygma, but ethical instruction is in every biblical sermon. Otherwise, cheap grace is preached.

C. H. Dodd, separating kerygma from didache too sharply as an academician, called the church to get the kerygma at the center of its preaching.[6] That is a proper emphasis in any era. But the distinction between preaching and teaching in the early church was not as sharp as Dodd implies. The functions of the preacher and the teacher were not compartmentalized in the life and work of the apostles. They preached and taught daily. To neglect either function of ministry is to be unfaithful to God. Jesus came preaching. He also came teaching; the common people heard him gladly (Mark 1:22). "You are a teacher sent from God," they said (John 3:2).

Evangelical teaching, which I have contrasted with lecturing (even on the Bible), is inseparable from biblical preaching. Both draw on and present the same content in different forms and with different emphases. If one addresses the decline of the preaching function in the church *and* the church's neglect of its magisterial function *and* the sell-out of pastoral counseling (from the resources of the Word) to psychological counseling, he or she will

be at the heart of the church's ineffective biblical witness
in modern society.

> Responsibility for teaching rests upon the whole
> church even though only certain members undertake
> specific teaching assignments, just as responsibility for
> the maintenance of the pure preaching of the gospel and
> the right observance of the sacraments rests upon the
> whole church, even though only a limited number of
> persons are called upon to preach or to dispense the
> sacraments.[7]

A sermon is not biblical until it is the means for God's
Word (law and gospel, didache and kerygma) *to divide
the congregation up into individuals,* persuading each to
decide for or against Christ.[8] Evangelical teaching does
that too.

> There is no such thing as a teaching sermon that is
> purely intellectual in its aim and results, nor can there
> be a sermon which is purely an emotional appeal; mere
> excitement, no matter how strong, dies leaving little
> behind it except a thirst for further excitement . . .
> there is always one thing more important than the at-
> tempt to move people, and that is the attempt to speak
> the truth in love.[9]

Christian preaching and teaching are directed to the
whole person—intellect, emotions, and will—to the human
imagination.[10] If a sermon is wholly intellectual or wholly
emotional or wholly hortatory, it is not biblical. Evangelical teaching and biblical preaching are inseparable functions of Christian ministry.

The sermon is not a sales pitch, a means for manipulat-
ing the hearers to undertake this or that task for the official board, the pastor, the denomination, or a worthy

community organization. In this era of blatant and subtle manipulation, harsh and gentle intimidation, violent and gentle coercion, there is heavy cultural pressure—ecclesiastical as well as secular—to turn the church's preachers into hucksters and manipulators. Biblical preaching is not a plea to buy a product. It is the announcement of God's gift of himself, an urgent plea to accept his gift, and an admonition to do his commandments. Biblical preaching is not the selling of Christ—like the selling of the Pentagon or a denominational appeal or program. It is the sharing of Christ with needy people who are impoverished spiritually and materially. Biblical preaching is the continuing activity of God. Revelation and response, promise and command, gift and invitation are at the heart of biblical preaching. The English Puritans emphasized God's sovereignty rather than his mercy, but they were not moralists. They spoke of God's demands as "commands with promise." The biblical preacher handles God's full counsel—law and gospel, demand and promise.

Biblical preaching does not sell, manipulate, or intimidate. God's deed-in-Christ is a divine imperative, but it does not coerce; it confronts. God's grace is free; it is not cheap. Essentially, it calls for faith in Christ and ethical decisions framed and motivated by God's amazing grace. Biblical preaching lays heavy demands on the whole person of the believer: (a) intellectual assent on critical grounds, (b) trust that Jesus reveals God as he is, and (c) obedience to Christ's commands. Christianity does not thrive on blind faith or self-serving affirmations. Sermons that plug peace of mind, huckster possibility thinking, foster a cultural piety, embrace civil religion uncritically, or endorse the religion of civility—and these pass as "good preaching" in too many American churches—are not essentially different from the medieval practice of selling indulgences. Reaction against the latter sparked personal and church renewal on a broad scale in the sixteenth century. The former seem to offend few and please many today.

A sermon is not a solo performance. The pulpit is the prow of the church/ship, the primary means of getting the gospel into confrontation with people, but it is not the whole ship. The pulpit is not a stage for the preacher to display his or her talents. My impression is that there was more "performing" and posturing in the pulpits on the American frontier from 1750-1890, and in English and American pulpits (especially in the large cities), 1870-1940, than there is today. We got away from the "Elmer Gantry" preachers after 1920 and the big-city "pulpiteers" after 1945, not only because the frontier had disappeared and the cities were becoming unsafe and unsavory to middle-class church people, but also because people had access to better "performers" in the entertainment and political worlds via electronic mass media—first radio and then television. Presently, however, television is bringing back a cadre of *religious* "performers." Privatistic religion feeds on their undemanding performances. Some pastors, at their wits end yet knowing better, succumb nonetheless to the temptation of emulating these TV "religious" performers, hoping to fill their empty churches. Some do, God forgive them. The biblical sermon is not a performance, and it certainly is not a solo performance.

The sermon, then, is not an essay, a public speech, a lecture, a sales pitch, or a solo performance.

There is another elemental difference between those forms of communication and the biblical sermon. Effective essayists, public speakers, lecturers, sales persons, re-

ligious performers, and news analysts do what they do
from human resources, their own and others. Their content is self-generated, situationally inspired, or "group"
prepared. The content of the biblical sermon is *given;* it
is not contrived, invented, or created by the preacher.
Some theologians and parish preachers appear to rely
mainly on their considerable talents and wide cultural
knowledge to provide the content of their work. But it is
not solidly biblical. A few of these communicate with
striking effectiveness. Now and then one turns out to be
a pied-piper. But these "preachers" are not *servants* of
God's Word. The effective biblical preacher does not cre-
ate his message; he or she is, as Bagehot said of Maurice,
the channel for it. When the preacher is *that,* and the
content is biblical, his or her sermon pleases God.

Dependence on God then is a distinctive mark of biblical preaching. God's messengers do not preach on their
own, because the life they live is not their own. Paul put
it this way: "Yet not I live, but Christ lives in me." Christian preaching is the work of the Holy Spirit through the
Word discerned by a particular man or woman who, in
response to God's call, prepares and proclaims it to persons-in-community to nurture their faith and empower
them to serve God in the world. Biblical preachers are
channels of the Word. They are Christ's ambassadors.
They give what they have first received. To be sure, their
attitude and bearing, style and structuring of sermons are
part of effective communication. But these personal at-
tributes and vocational skills are also harnessed to reveal
the Christ who lives in them. Biblical preachers testify
to God's mighty deeds in history as recorded in the Scriptures, in the course of history, *and* in their own experience. "The unique fact about preaching is that which is

behind the preacher—the reality of a God who speaks. Any discussion of preaching that does not begin there might as well not begin at all." [11]

We have prepared the way for this final observation about the biblical sermon. As the preacher does not stand alone, the biblical sermon does not stand alone. It is one significant strand among other significant strands in the corporate experience of God's people who have assembled in a particular place, at a pre-arranged hour around the Word in preaching, teaching, sacraments, and fellowship. They have come together—eighty or two hundred or twelve hundred—to praise and thank God with hymns and Psalms and prayers, to make a humble confession of their sins and accept gratefully his healing forgiveness in the biblical words of absolution, to receive his promises and to open themselves to his commands, to pray for themselves and all manner and conditions of people, to participate hungrily at Christ's table, and to hear his Word to them in that place and hour.[12] The *biblical* sermon is an *act* of worship by *pastor and people*.

In biblical preaching, the proclaimer offers his person and work to the high and holy God, asking that both shall be joined together as an effective vehicle for God's truth in that particular hour of worship. God's people in corporate worship also offer themselves to him as they open their hearts and minds and wills to his Word in liturgy, preaching, and sacraments. Christian worship is a voluntary response to God's grace, an act of obedient freedom to his demands, and a joyous celebration of the new life in Christ. It is not an escape from the world. It is not a rule of safety. It is instead a risky deed, for worship and witness and service to others are of a piece. Stephen and Peter dared to worship God; they died because of it. Tertullian and Augustine dared to worship God; they suffered for it.

Luther and Calvin dared to worship God; they were impoverished for it. Kaj Munk, Bonhoeffer, and King dared to worship God; they were killed for it. The worship of Yahweh, the Father of Abraham and Jacob and David and Jesus, is not a retreat from life but a gathering of his resources to meet life boldly as a person and in the company of like-minded persons to work at building a just society in one's own place and time.

In Christian worship, the biblical sermon is part of the whole through which God's Word reaches for embodiment in each worshiper until it becomes a deed in the church, community, nation, and world. When this happens, the worship service—as plain as a Mennonite order or as rich in tradition and symbolism as the Greek Orthodox order—is Christian worship. Worship is a natural human response to some god or other—mate, child, possessions, power, a political leader, Allah, Jehovah, the Father of our Lord, Jesus Christ. The psalmist, yearning after Yahweh, cried out that his heart thirsted for God as the deer pants for the cool mountain stream. In the fourth Christian century Augustine wrote: "We are restless till we find our rest in Thee." This is what an earlier church father, Tertullian, meant, I think, when he said that we are "naturally Christian." We were fashioned to worship the true God even as the Prodigal Son was fashioned to return home and live as a son should.

So worship is not only an act that praises and glorifies God for what he has done in Christ, but on the human level it is also a joyous celebration of the new life in Christ. Worship and true community (koinonia) go hand-in-hand in the experience of prodigals who come home and are reunited in the Father's household. They celebrate this new estate, grateful that they were bought for a price, the precious blood of their Lord and Savior, Jesus Christ;

and dignified as persons because they were bought for a purpose—doing God's work in the world.

It is into the midst of God's gathered people in congregations everywhere that preachers enter, themselves worshipers too. But they are always aware of the human presumption that sets them off from the other worshipers, for they themselves are anticipated to be a part of whatever God accomplishes there that day! What a saving grace, then, that in those gathered companies before preachers speak their words for God, the Lord of heaven and cosmos speaks his Word through the ancient witness to them. Biblical preachers confess their deep-set sin and unworthiness. They hear the words of absolution, are assured of their acceptibility, and accept God's many-splendored acts of grace. Through a Christian liturgy, their "appointed" place in God's total plan of redemption is delineated. Faith calls unto faith, and the most weary, plodding preacher is lifted up to speak God's Word that day. It is more than enough to challenge every herald of God's Word to appear with nothing less than his or her best, and, in God's strength, to do more than his or her best.

Christian worship rests on God's-deed-in-Christ. It is edifying for the faith of the beloved community and essential to its mission in the world. Christian worship is not cultic by nature. It takes place in the cultural context of the congregation. It is rooted in the faith and life and work of the people in that place. It is properly ordered, as Paul put it, when it allows God's Spirit freedom to operate among the people who are assembled to worship. Christian worship is not an escape from the world. It is "the responsible service of those that have put their hand to the plow and have not looked back, but with burning hearts join in the cry, 'Maranatha, our Lord, come.'" [13]

In the hour of Christian worship the drama of salvation is reenacted with the worshipers—pastors and people—as participants, loved and therefore loving, understood and therefore understanding, receiving and therefore giving, served and therefore serving. For preaching, teaching, and sacraments; healing, evangelizing, and committee meetings; Bible study, stewardship, and parish administration are not only means whereby the Word confronts people, but equally the means of encouraging saved sinners to worship the Lord and Father of us all, which is, in effect, to join in his Son's ministry in and to the world.

Wherever the church exercises fully its prophetic, teaching, pastoral, priestly, and diaconic functions, it gets up to its steeple in politics and economics and social action. God is interested in more than religion! The cross of Christ was raised in the world. As George McLeod reminds us, Jesus was not crucified on a golden cross on an ornate altar between two golden candlesticks. He was crucified on the hillside of a stone quarry used for burials outside the city wall of Jerusalem.[14] The church exists to serve Christ in the world where people barter their souls for power, scuttle their self-respect for economic reward, surrender their integrity for illicit relationships, and kill each other with sophisticated weapons or use food for sovereign gain. Worship and witness are inseparable. Biblical preaching and evangelical teaching are at the heart of both.

When Bernard Malamud was honored at the National Book Awards ceremony in 1967, he quoted Herman Melville: "To produce a mighty book you must choose a mighty theme." Biblical preachers have the mightiest theme in human history—God was in Christ reconciling the world to himself. It is the church's responsibility to get that deed of reconciliation into the lives of church members and, through them, into the world. Unless this saving truth is at the heart of each sermon, the sermon is not biblical even though the preacher announces a text, comments knowledgeably on a long biblical passage, or analyzes insightfully the tangled roots of racial injustice. From first to last, biblical preaching sounds the note: "God was in Christ reconciling the world unto himself" —and pleads urgently, "Be reconciled to God."

There have been preachers from Apollos in Corinth to the TV religious hucksters of our day who, having developed a preaching style and a formula for "success" attractive to a certain mind-set, are effective in members counted and monies collected. Their imitators in the parish do rather well in some parts of the United States because they attract and cater to lay people who, from their abundance and their narcissistic needs, finance these "successful" churches that buttress a social-economic status quo that favors them. These ministers and their congregations are convinced, as Jesus predicted, that they are serving God. Recruited and ordained by an uncritical church, these "hirelings" and their lay "masters" hold the same creed: "After me, the deluge." But perceptive people in and outside the church know that this brand of people-pleasing, success-oriented preaching deserves Huckleberry Finn's evaluation of his one half-hearted effort to pray: "Nothin' come of it." It was *this* preaching that led Peter Berger to observe two decades ago that preaching has no effect on lay people the other six days of the week.[15]

What is a biblical sermon? It is the story of Jesus and his love told by one who knows he or she is loved and therefore loves in return, told persuasively in the cultural images and idiom of his or her hearers so that they, assembled to worship God, learn again that they are loved

by God, can love him in return, and from the resources
of his love are empowered to reach out to help hurting
people in their intimate fellowship and in the world. A
biblical sermon is God's message of liberation from sin,
demonic powers, and death communicated through the
person of the preacher to persons in the community of
faith and through them to persons and social institutions
in the world. The Message—God was in Christ reconciling
the world to himself—is most effective when it is proclaimed by a messenger who is himself or herself responding wholeheartedly to God's revelation of his gracious
will.

When Peter and John, imprisoned for healing disabled
people, were released miraculously, an angel of the Lord
instructed them: "Go . . . tell the people all about this
new life" (Acts 5:20 GNB). Biblical sermons are the telling
and retelling of God's liberating deed in Jesus of Nazareth, of his yearning that every human return to his household, of his gift of new life in Christ, of his power to put
people on their feet for time and eternity, and of his eager-
ness to fashion a just society here and now. This good
news is at the heart of biblical preaching. It makes the
sermon uniquely different from all other forms of writing
and speaking. "Go tell the people," says Ferris, "that the
life that is in Christ Jesus may be in them."[16] And tell
them too, that, as they were bought for a price—the precious blood of Christ—they were bought for a purpose,
to do his work in the world. This is the nature and purpose of biblical preaching.

In the next chapter we shall examine how biblical
preachers structure their sermons.

8 The Sermon: Its Structure

> The power of a sermon (given its content) lies in its structure, not in its decoration.
> —Halford Luccock

LOVE OF CHRIST AND GLAD OBEDIENCE TO HIS CALL provide the reasons for our preaching. Concern for people, informed by and conformed to God's rightful claim on them, provides the relational context in which we preach. Church traditions, national traditions, and community mores comprise part of the historical (time-oriented) context in which we preach. God's Word is what we preach. Given all four conditions reasonably met, we still shall not preach effectively until we learn to structure and clothe sermons so that they bring the Word and the congregation face-to-face. It is in that historical-existential context that individuals say yes or no to Christ.

The preacher—like the poet and the novelist, the musical composer and the artist—values structure and form. C. S. Lewis put it this way: "It is easy to forget that the man who writes a good love sonnet need not only be enamored of a woman but also be enamored of the sonnet." [1] Structure and form are as crucial to effective sermon-making as they are to writing good poetry and composing durable music. A century before Christ, Cicero observed that an effective public address interests, instructs, and motivates the hearers. Effective biblical preaching interests people in Jesus, instructs them in God's promises and demands, and motivates them to take up their cross and follow Christ. Structure is essential if a sermon is to be an effective means through which God's Spirit accomplishes these aims.

Some clergy ignore structure; others insist that it cannot be taught. D. Martyn Lloyd-Jones—a conservative, Spirit-filled preacher at Westminster Chapel, London (1940-1970)—speaks against the view that it can be taught. He declares dogmatically that "preachers are born not made. . . . You will never teach a man to be a preacher," he thunders, "if he is not already one." [2] Lloyd-Jones' book on preaching is ruggedly honest, often insightful, sometimes soaring in spirit. But he is badly off course in arguing that "preachers are born, not made." After all, sinners must be born again, made over, grow in the likeness of Christ. Theodore Ferris is closer to the experience of most preachers when he observes that "sincere men without the gift of genius can become *good* (effective) preachers by training and effort." [3] Effective preachers are not born to the vocation; they must *learn* to preach effectively. Formal and informal teaching is part of this lifelong learning process.

Certainly, no crafter of sermons can establish precisely how another ought to do his sermon-making. But there are basic guidelines that save the beginner from disaster and, reviewed periodically by experienced preachers, keep the veteran at the necessary business of learning how to preach more effectively. From a quarter-century of teaching homiletics and reading sermons Halford Luccock observed that too many sermons "splatter gelatinously around the four walls of the church" for want of a skeletal outline. The experienced preacher knows how easily that disaster can happen. The beginning preacher is scarcely aware when it does happen!

All teachers of expository writing insist on a thesis before the student begins to write his or her paper, doctoral dissertation, story, or book. Unless *you* know what you want to say, and can set it down concisely, it is not likely that your hearers will know either. My own practice is to set down in a brief outline and in a paragraph or two the substance of the sermon I intend to preach. Ordinarily, in parish preaching, I set down a tentative outline some weeks ahead of time, but the final outline usually comes out of working with a particular sermon for ten hours or so. I think as I write. But I always work from a thesis statement. I produce twenty or more sermons in rough outline during the summer months, discarding some along the way, but keeping ahead on the preaching schedule throughout the year.

Both directives, a working outline and a precis, should be followed faithfully throughout one's ministry. This directive will be violated occasionally when one has learned how to preach effectively, but only when other legitimate parish work devours the week. In the preacher's early years, the outline should be evident to the hearers. Theodore P. Ferris, a distinguished Episcopal preacher, 1930-1972, and a part-time teacher of preachers for three decades, offered this sane counsel:

> In the beginning, the form of the sermon will doubtless be as obvious as the clothesline on which the clothes hang. Better to have the line visible than have the clothes go on the ground in a heap. . . . As time goes on the form will be more skillfully clothed with garments of

meaning. It will still be there like the steel framework
of a building, but it will be clothed so that the listeners
may be scarcely aware of its presence.[4]

A sermon divided into more than three or four parts
tends, however, to be overblown in intent and under-
nourished in content; and it is likely to get out of hand
when it is preached. I remember a student in one of my
graduate preaching seminars at Lancaster Theological
Seminary in the middle 1960s—an experienced, competent
workman for the Lord. He preached a seven-point sermon
in a practice preaching session. Every point was relevant
to his text, each point was developed concisely, each point
marched resolutely into the next. Nonetheless, his class-
mates and I agreed that it was too much. The sermon was
over-structured, over-prepared, and overwhelming. It reminded me of Clemenceau's caustic comment on Wilson's
Fourteen Points for making peace in the world: "The
good Lord had only ten points; Wilson has fourteen!"
Wilson wanted to make a better world in a single generation. Clemenceau was concerned only to secure France
against Germany for the next generation. Both failed.
Wilson attempted too much; Clemenceau attempted too
little. Both faults victimize many preachers and account
for thousands of ineffective sermons—too much or too
little.

Preparing sermons, no less than writing novels or poetry, painting or composing music, requires strict attention to form and structure. Preaching that reaches out to
us from earlier generations is structured. Here are several
examples.

Arthur John Gossip, in one of the most poignant gospel
sermons of this century titled, "When Life Tumbles In,
What Then?" [5]—preached after his wife's unexpected and

sudden death—hung his soaring witness on a simple two-part structure that is apparent only after careful examination. It is skillfully clothed with garments of meaning. But the structure is there. Gossip first traced in vivid detail how everyone comes to his time of testing; then, he demonstrated how one who holds to Christ is brought to solid ground. Gossip's biblical content, the dramatic occasion, his luminous faith, and his gift for the right words made that sermon especially effective. But preachers would not be reading it today if it had not been well structured. The gifted preacher, Alexander Maclaren, preached three-part sermons so consistently that he won this accolade for his preaching: "He fed the sheep with a three-pronged fork." Whether the sermon is two, three, or four-pronged, the accolade, "fed the sheep," is every preacher's highest human award, second only to Jesus' "well done. . . ."

On the other hand, Thomas Chalmers did not preach with clear-cut divisions. He played variations on a single theme, as his famous sermon, "The Expulsive Power of a New Affection," demonstrates.[6] But that is structure—variations on a single theme. Musicians use it often. Haydn taught it to his students, Mozart and Beethoven. Frederick Robertson had another way of structuring a sermon that some preachers use occasionally when their congregations have been shaped by solid biblical-theological preaching. The Brighton preacher, having chosen a text for its variety, proceeded to develop his sermon in terms of two balancing truths. A good example is his sermon on "The Irreparable Past" (Mark 14:41-52). Robertson dealt first with "the irreparable past," and second with "the available future."

Since content often fashions its own form if the preacher works hard to let it happen, there are some fundamental observations that apply to structuring sermons well.

First, a sermon structure is sound when it allows the sermon to hang together easily, carries God's message understandably to the hearers, and aids the pastor in preaching it. If it will not "preach" readily, it is badly structured. Looking back over last week's sermon, the preacher can discern whether it hung together, carried the message intelligibly, and preached well. If it measures up on all three counts, it had good structure. If it does not, the structure was faulty.

Second, if the sermon hangs together, carries the message so clearly that it is understood by people whose minds and hearts are open, then the structure is not only sound but it has unity. Unity means "of a piece." It means that a sermon treats a single theme, avoids extraneous material, keeps the hearers' minds from running like sheep into byways while it is being preached.

Third, in well structured sermons—if the outline is intended "to show"—the "points" will march steadily forward, each point moving into the next as the two, three, or four points march steadily toward a common purpose. This often means the difference between effective and ineffective preaching. Gossip's two points take one steadily to the sermon's magnificent conclusion. Robertson's two points are balanced: point and counterpoint. Chalmers' variations are on a *single* theme; no other theme is introduced. Good sermon structure, like a sound human skeleton, has the necessary parts—no more, no less. Each part fits into the other parts allowing the sermon to accomplish its intended purpose.

Fourth, a mark of good structure—and poets, novelists, and musical composers agree—is symmetry. My thesaurus provides these meanings of symmetry: proportion, order, shapeliness, balance. Lincoln's Gettysburg Address has symmetry. It hangs together, marches toward its purpose without breaking stride, has no superfluous words, is marked by shapeliness and evenness. Paul's essay on faith, hope, and love has perfect symmetry. Most of the Psalms have a beautiful symmetry, especially in the King James translation. The first three chapters of Genesis and the prolog to the Gospel of John have magnificent symmetry. Jesus' parables are structured perfectly. Serious preachers study Lincoln and Milton, Paul and Genesis, John's Gospel and Jesus' parables for symmetry in writing and speech.[7]

Sermon structure also depends on the *kind* of sermon. the pastor intends to preach and its specific purpose. If the preacher is constrained by God's Word to alert his people to their nation's immoral course in a particular war, he or she will set out to speak prophetically (*for* God *against* a particular wrong decision or course of action or situation). If, on the other hand, the preacher wants to instruct and encourage his people in Christian family living, he or she will fashion a solid teaching sermon with therapeutic strands running through it. The kind of sermon one preaches determines its content, structure, emphases, and the preacher's style in preaching it.

Are there different kinds of sermons? If so, how does one identify or classify them? In theological school, I was taught—like others in my generation—that there are four kinds: textual, expository, doctrinal, and topical. One of my professors also brought to our attention Harry Emerson Fosdick's call for and practice of "life-situation" preaching. He enabled us to recognize that Fosdick was talking about introductions that begin where people are and preaching that is existential. I thought then—and still do—that Fosdick, working without a text, was more biblical and doctrinal than some of his critics and detractors. Nonetheless, I discovered that Fosdick's prescribed approach, if used exclusively, could lead an uncritical student of the Scriptures away from rather than into biblical preaching. A. J. Gossip guided me: "Dr. Fosdick is reported to have said that the business of the man in the pulpit is to preach on what is real and pressing to his hearers' minds. An excellent counsel, up to a point. But it is only a half truth. And half truths are, proverbially, dangerous." [8]

The biblical preacher is in fact compelled to begin often with God rather than a life situation and point out where the people should be if they want seriously to know Christ. In varying degrees, all congregations are biblically illiterate and theologically ignorant of the meaning and significance of revelation and history. The only serious contact many church members have with "revelation and history" is in the biblical-confessional preaching and teaching at Sunday morning worship services, in Sunday church school seminars, and in responsibly-led Bible study groups.

Searching out ways to preach relevantly, I learned early (1952) from Theodore Ferris to categorize my sermons broadly as *prophetic* (confrontational-in-freedom), *didactic* (expository, doctrinal, or ethical), *evangelical* (focused emphasis on the many facets of witnessing), and *therapeutic* (supportive, healing).[9] I added a fifth kind of sermon: *affirmational* (simple, strong statements of the fundamentals of the faith). All categories, however, must be undergirded by the spirit of proclamation (the law and gospel) or that particular "type" of sermon will not be biblical. A prophetic sermon degenerates into an emotional discharge of the preacher's opinions without biblical content *and* the spirit of proclamation. An expository sermon becomes an exercise in academics and an evangelical sermon an exercise in self-affirmation if proclamation of the strong simple statements of faith are not fundamental to each type. A therapeutic sermon plugs into absorption with personal needs, or leads to deification of self-centeredness if the sermon does not communicate the nature and mission of Jesus Christ. And an affirmational sermon, lacking the spirit of proclamation, becomes a lackluster reiteration of biblical themes or events locked in another time and place.

These categories made sense to me on the firing line of the American parish in the early 1950s. They still do. The preacher is on the way to preparing and preaching an effective sermon when he or she has a clear notion whether the central thrust and dominant accent of his or her message for the next Sunday is prophetic, didactic, largely evangelical, therapeutic, or affirmational. Flexibly employed, these broad categories are useful to preachers.

A twenty-five minute sermon that addresses the present balance of nuclear terror with biblical insight can include all these accents at the same time. It could also be wholly prophetic or wholly didactic or substantially therapeutic. It could not be *wholly* evangelical because of the content, structure, and style. A biblical sermon on human nature could be expository (story of Jacob or Jeremiah or Peter) or doctrinal; that is, it could be didactic. It could also be largely evangelical or wholly therapeutic. It could not be, I think, wholly prophetic. A sermon that addresses human anxiety could be largely therapeutic or substantially didactic. It could not be wholly prophetic or totally evangelical. A sermon on the fifteenth chapter of Luke (the parables of the Lost Sheep, the Lost Coin, the Prodigal Son, and the Elder Brother) could be wholly didactic (expository) or wholly evangelical or wholly therapeutic or wholly prophetic. A sermon on John 3:16 could be any one of the five or all five in one. A sermon on John 11—"I am the Resurrection . . ."—could also be any one of the five or all five in one; so could sermons based on 1 Corinthians 13, John 14, Matthew 18:16, Matthew 5, 6, and 7, and so on.

A sermon that begins with a text is not automatically biblical. Running patter, verse-by-verse, on a passage of Scripture is not expository preaching. On the other hand, a topical sermon on racial discrimination which sets forth a point of view and a spirit grounded in God's Word is biblical. A sermon on the doctrine of the Incarnation may be "doctrinal" in a technical sense, but unless the hearers are brought face-to-face with God-in-man (Jesus), it is a theological discourse, not a biblical sermon. Unless a therapeutic sermon on apathy, for example, brings God's healing, it is not, in spite of its valid psychological insights, a biblical sermon. It is a psychological address. A teaching sermon on the doctrine of the Trinity that fails to enlarge the hearers' understanding of one God in three Persons so that they thank him for creation and sustenance, accept his liberating deed-in-Christ, and respond to the promptings of his Spirit, is not a biblical sermon. It is a lecture on doctrine.

Of course, it matters little how one classifies sermons if the Word of the Lord—biblically rooted, enriched by the church's understanding of it, enlivened by the preacher's experience of it, and cast in secular language—does not come through the person of the preacher to the persons of the hearers so that they say yes or no to Christ. Biblical preaching is as elemental as that, and as difficult.

But this does not excuse any preacher from structuring carefully every sermon for clarity, insight, challenge, support, condemnation, healing, promise, and assurance. Use the classifications if they are helpful. If not, remember this: a well structured sermon, like good poetry and good music, adheres to its type. It knows what it wants to accomplish, sets out to do it with singleness of purpose, and does it.

Here is the outline (structure) of an effective biblical sermon. It was preached by Martin Luther King, 1929-1968, to his congregation in Montgomery, Alabama, in the mid-1950s. At the time, he was less than thirty years of age. In it, one sees the bold biblical preacher of the late 1950s and the 1960s coming to maturity. There *are* seminarians and young pastors who preach biblically and veteran pastors who rarely do.

Title: **Our God Is Able**[10]

Text: "Now unto him that is able to keep you from falling"—Jude 24.

Introduction

"At the center of the Christian Faith is the conviction that in the universe there is a God of power who is able to do exceedingly abundant things in nature and in history...."

I

Let us notice, first, that God is able to sustain the vast scope of the physical universe. Here again, we are tempted to feel that man is the true master of the physical universe....

II

Let us notice that God is able to subdue all the powers of evil. In affirmation that God is able to conquer evil we admit the reality of evil. Christianity has never dismissed evil as illusory, or an error of the mortal mind. . . .

III

Let us notice, finally, that God is able to give us interior resources to confront the trials and difficulties of life. Each of us faces circumstances in life which compel us to carry heavy burdens of sorrow. Adversity assails us with hurricane force. . . .

King's conclusion to his sermon was exceptionally long. It was effective, nonetheless, because he ushered his hearers into the secret recesses of his being, revealing how he—exhausted by vicious phone calls and frightened by threats against his family—finally, decisively turned everything over to God who sustained him then and, King declared, would sustain him in the years ahead. And God did.

When the American author, William Dean Howells, first read Tolstoy, he declared: "I can never again see life in the way I saw it before I knew him." One's preaching is truly biblical, solidly structured, appealingly styled, and effectively proclaimed when parishioners say, "Our minister enables us to see Christ, and seeing him, we can never again see life the way we saw it before." If that is to be said of your preaching and mine, we shall, given the basics, need to learn to structure our sermons so that they have symmetry, unity, forward movement, and maximum impact on the human mind, emotions, and will. Jesus did say that we should love the Lord our God with all our mind, all our heart, and all our strength.

Moved by the Spirit to preach on a particular biblical truth for a particular purpose to a particular congregation, and having structured and clothed God's truth in the images and idiom of those particular people, the preacher has yet to fashion an introduction that launches the sermon quickly and cleanly, a conclusion that brings it to port soundly and safely, and a title that is inviting, memorable, and honest. Those are the themes of the next chapter.

9 The Sermon: Its Introduction, Conclusion, and Title

The devils enter uninvited when the house stands empty. For other kinds of guests, you have first to open the door.
—Dag Hammarskjold, *Markings.*

MERICANS GO TO THE THEATER to be entertained, to the university to be educated, to a daily job to make a livelihood, and to the beach, the mountains, Las Vegas, and the Alps for recreation. But they must shift their intellectual and emotional gears hard to hear the Word—and harder still to do it. In the congregation's unconscious mind, cultural weaknesses (anti-intellectualism, anti-authority, and anti-tradition attitudes) militate against hearing the Word with understanding. Because of human sin, all people resist God's truth even when they need and seek it. They have the capacity to pursue and experience truth, but no one is easily inclined to do it.

An effective introduction will command the attention of the congregation immediately without cheapening the message. That is a weighty assignment for one who preaches once or twice a week for years in the same parish. But it need not be crushing. The preacher is not

143

required—as TV producers are—to devise a dramatic introduction week after week, each more stunning than the last, something "out of this world." Indeed, if the introduction to the sermon is out of this world, overly dramatic or bizzare, it will not interest the hearers. And if it is not germane to the sermon's content, it will lessen the impact of that sermon and weaken the preacher's credibility.

In clergy circles, one of the best known examples of a dramatic introduction to a sermon was provided by Sparhawk Jones, preaching years ago at Princeton University. He took for his text, 2 Kings 8:13, "Is Thy servant a dog that he should do this?" Having read the text, he paused for dramatic effect, and said, "Well, dog or no dog, he did it." Paul Scherer, relating the story, observed that Jones' arresting introduction had nothing to do with a sound interpretation of that text. The man's sermon was wrong-headed from first to last![1] Do not try to be clever in shaping the introduction. Let the introduction be honest, accurate, brief; get to the body of the sermon quickly. One of the most effective biblical preachers in the history of the church, John Chrysostom (354-407), frequently got to the body of his sermon so quickly that he was abrupt.[2]

Low-key introductions are in order. In a teaching sermon on the church as people living together in Christ, the parish pastor can begin as simply as this: "Today, we want to talk about our life together in Jesus Christ," and get on with his sermon. Walter J. Burghardt, professor at Catholic University and a member of the Woodstock Theological Center, began an address at the Notre Dame Center for Pastoral Liturgy in these words:

> Some years ago, at old Woodstock College in Maryland, I was plagued by a bothersome rhetorical problem.

> I had just about finished an Easter homily, but I was-dissatisfied. So I walked down the corridor to the room of my learned colleague and dear friend, John Courtney Murray. I told him: "John, I need your help. This Easter sermon here—I have my usual three points, and I have my conclusion. But I don't have an introduction." I was thinking, of course, in terms of a startling opening story, an attention-grabber. Murray looked at me for a moment, then said quietly and simply: "Walter, why don't you tell them what you're going to talk about?" [3]

That is precisely what Professor Burghardt did. It is a sound, honest, effective way to introduce a sermon.

On the other hand, Elton Trueblood, one of the most effective teaching preachers in his generation, introduced his influential sermon on "The Yoke of Christ" (Matt. 11:29-30), in a more descriptive fashion:

> It is not easy to be a human being. Human life carries with it marvelous possibilities of fulfillment, but there are, at the same time, untold ways in which it can go wrong. . . .
> The universality of human sorrow and need is one of the reasons for the great attractiveness of the words of Jesus which appear at the end of the eleventh chapter of Matthew. When Jesus said, 'Come unto Me, all ye who labor and are heavy laden,' he is really speaking to all. . . .
> Another reason for the attractiveness of these sentences is the fact that they include Christ's clearest call to commitment to be found in all the gospels. . . .[4]

One can scarcely improve on Trueblood's contextual, life-centered introduction. Notice especially his lead sentence—nine simple words: "It is not easy to be a human being." That sticks with the hearer not because it is clever, but because it is true.

Harry Emerson Fosdick, speaking on the high cost of

human freedom, had his sermon off the runway in a single paragraph:

> A Spanish proverb runs, "Take what you want, says God, take it and pay for it." That proverb does not cover the whole of life; some of our experience is beyond the scope of our choice; we have to take, whether we choose or not. But at the center of life there is an area of personal selection where we pick and choose between alternatives, and where God does say to each of us, "Take what you want, take and pay for it." [5]

I introduced a sermon titled, "Does Prayer Make Any Difference?" in a biblical context because it was a teaching sermon.

> James identified one cause of human trouble, personal and social, when he said, "You have not, because you ask not." Paul, shepherding the young church, urged his fellow pilgrims "to pray without ceasing." James also reminded them that the prayers of "a righteous man" are effective.
>
> Jesus himself relied heavily on prayer. Often as the Judean sun sank across the western hills, he knelt in some secluded place; and as the sun rose the next morning across the land of Moab, he rose from his all-night rendezvous with God. Jesus prayed on every occasion: at his baptism, when he faced temptation, before choosing his disciples, before performing miracles. He prayed for little children, the sick, the dying, the lost, his disciples, his family, his enemies. Jesus prayed in people's homes, on the road, in the fields, in the marketplace, on the Sea of Galilee, in the synagogue, and in the Temple. Faced with Calvary, he retired to Gethsemane to pray. His resolve strengthened in prayer, he accepted the Cross. His last breath on Calvary was a simple prayer: "Father, into your hands I commit my spirit."
>
> This morning we shall examine three areas of human experience in which prayer *does* make a difference: in

the natural world, in meeting and handling life's inevitable situational tensions, and in discerning and doing God's will.

The length of the introduction to a sermon is determined by the subject to be dealt with; the congregation's knowledge of the text or Scripture passage, doctrine, issue, or problem to be addressed; and the congregation's general biblical knowledge, cultural sophistication, and level of commitment to Christ. Even so, the introduction to most sermons should be brief. It should *introduce* what the preacher intends to say.

A sermon I preached recently, "Why Do We Behave the Way We Do?" was introduced in four simple, declarative sentences. "Man has always been his own most vexing problem. On that note, Reinhold Niebuhr launched his Gifford Lectures forty years ago. But one need not be a professional theologian to share Niebuhr's judgment on human nature. Each of us has lived long enough with himself and herself and other selves to know first-hand how vexing any self, one's own and others', can be." The body of the sermon focused on (1) sin as separation from God; (2) the grandeur and misery in being human; and (3) the new set of affections Christ provides.

John Henry Jowett, a remarkably effective biblical preacher on both sides of the Atlantic in the early twentieth century, began a sermon titled, "The Wonders of Redemption" (Gal. 2:10)—"I have been crucified with Christ. . . ."), in this elemental way:

> What shall we do with this passage? How shall we approach it? Shall we come to it as agents or as controversialists, as suppliants or as combatants? . . . I would approach it as a guest and not as a soldier. I come to feast and not to fight.[6]

From that beginning, which introduced his message
compellingly, Jowett preached one of his characteristically
poetic sermons on the meaning of redemption through
Jesus Christ. Look again at Jowett's question: "What shall
we do with this passage?" When that simple question is
put honestly to a congregation about a soaring text not
easily understood, it draws the congregation as a magnet
draws iron filings; they participate at once. Of course, one
will employ this kind of introduction sparingly. In careless hands, it could be disastrous if the preacher, having
put the question, demonstrates in the following twenty-
five minutes that he does not know what to do with it.

Merrill Abbey observed that "life moving openings" can
be achieved through these five strategies. The preacher
may begin with (1) a situation, (2) something that
makes a crucial difference, (3) an effect needing a cause,
(4) something startling, or (5) a conflict.[7]

To Abbey's five strategies for introducing sermons, I
shall add two others. The first is this. One can begin
eschatologically rather than historically and work back.
The kingdom of God is a present task; it is also a future
hope. We work for it, but we also wait patiently for its
full coming. If we do not keep *that* before our people and
ourselves both they and we will go down, short of the
kingdom, because we shall lose hope. Christian hope is
defined luminously in the resurrected Christ and solidly
in various parts of the gospels, epistles, the books of Revelation, Daniel, Jonah, and Hosea; in the three creeds of
Christendom; in the doctrines of Christ's second coming,
final judgment, and completion of his work; in God's new
heaven and earth; and in the current rash of "theologies
of hope." Biblical preachers carry a large strand of eschatology in their preaching; otherwise it would not be fully
biblical. Jesus' "Sermon on the Mount" (a collection of

his teachings on various occasions) is eschatological, historical, and existential. If we lose the eschatological dimension of God's Word, we shall caricature the historical and existential dimensions of Christ's life and work. This loss is a major fault in much contemporary preaching; it is *so* mundane. Without those soaring promises—Christ will give us the kingdom, wipe away all tears, come again in power and glory—the gospel is not fully preached.

The second strategy is more specific: begin with God's statement (text, biblical passage, whole book of the Bible) to the human situation: What did God say then? Why? What is he saying now? What does he expect us to do? How shall we go about doing it? What power does he provide? Do not back away from doctrinal preaching. Take the essence of a church doctrine (incarnation, original sin), and apply it to the human condition. Properly done, Bible-centered and doctrinal preaching *is* "life situation" preaching.

In fashioning effective introductions there is only one elemental rule to remember: the introduction *introduces* the hearers to the subject and, explicitly or implicitly, identifies the purpose of the sermon. Charles Spurgeon offered good counsel for getting the attention of the congregation: "Give your hearers something which they can treasure up and remember." [8] That also focuses attention where it belongs: on the message, not the medium. The preacher will never begin with a personal reference unless it is as illustrative of the faith as Arthur John Gossip's or as witty and germane to the material and the occasion as was Adlai Stevenson's introduction to his remarks at a press conference the morning after his defeat for the Presidency in 1952: "A funny thing happened to me on the way to the White House." [9]

The introduction creates interaction with the congregation as it sets forth the subject and purpose of a particular sermon. It launches the sermon into the congregation and launchings, both of ships and sermons, should be clean, free, and quick.[10] If an interesting introduction is not possible now and again, do not fret or waste valuable time trying to devise one. Simply begin by saying, "This morning we shall consider obedience to God . . . the nature of faith, . . . the meaning of the sacraments, . . . injustice toward the minorities in Lancaster," and so on. Then do well what you promised to do.

THE CONCLUSION

If the introduction should launch the sermon cleanly, quickly, and freely, the conclusion should end it with equal dispatch. But the conclusion carries a larger burden than the introduction. One can, and often does, begin a sermon low-key, sometimes sluggishly, warming up as he or she gets into the sermon. That is not ideal; neither is it disastrous. A solid sermon will overmatch a dull beginning, even an inept beginning. But a weak or rambling conclusion will reduce the impact of a strong sermon or turn a weak sermon into a total loss.

The conclusion to the sermon *is* crucial. It is the last impression the preacher makes in a particular sermon. If it fizzles, comes off abruptly, is irrelevant to what has been said, the impact of the sermon will be blunted. If the practical purpose of preaching is to make people aware of Christ's love for them, to move them to take up a responsible stewardship of the gospel, to persuade them to bring their Christian insights to bear on particular social and political issues, then the conclusion must be prepared carefully and spoken persuasively to fix in the minds, hearts, and wills of the hearers the content and the purpose of the sermon.

Most preachers have difficulty with conclusions. More often than they care to remember, they have missed the proper moment to conclude and leave the pulpit. Effective conclusions are extremely difficult to write. They are even harder to manage in the act of preaching. And, like the body of the sermon, they are preached in an emotional, intellectual context that is not precisely predictable in the preacher's study or when beginning his or her sermon. The mind-set of the congregation has changed during the preceding twenty-five minutes of preaching. The congregation's emotional and intellectual receptiveness has opened or closed in that time, subject to many impulses other than the sermon. That is also true of the preacher's mind and feelings. Both congregation and preacher at the end of twenty-five minutes of preaching will have a decidedly different attitude from that which each had at the beginning of the sermon. The last several minutes of the sermon, therefore, are crucial in nailing down what is positive or in retrieving what may otherwise be lost.[11]

Luther opined that the time to end a sermon is "when you see your hearers are most attentive. . . ." But most sermon-hearers in American congregations are courteous and long-suffering. They do not whistle, clap, issue catcalls, or stomp as some worshipers did in earlier centuries. In fact, few American lay people ever criticize their preacher's sermons to him or her. Polite attentiveness, a tuned-out mind, is characteristic of white middle-class congregations where the preaching is dull. Presently, the American way of protest is non-verbal: sporadic attendance or Christmas-Easter attendance. Luther's observation was relevant in sixteenth-century Germany. It is not particularly helpful in casual, pious, white middle-class

American congregations in the twilight years of the twentieth century.

There is another limitation in Luther's counsel for preaching in our era. Preachers are indeed obliged to respect the sensibilities of their people. They are also *obligated* to present God's message in-depth. Luther would agree. Many church members today have to be educated to listen to biblical preaching. In time, many of these come to hunger and thirst after God's Word. But this congregational attitude requires years of cultivation through effective biblical preaching and evangelical teaching, serious dialog about the nature and purpose of preaching, and faithful pastoral work. There have been times over the years at Trinity when both the congregation and I would have preferred to close a sermon ten minutes earlier to avoid the tough applications of God's Word to specific situations in Trinity, Lancaster, and the nation. But to have done so would have denied them and me the Word of God which is always personal, communal, specific, concrete. When to conclude a particular sermon depends not only on the sensibilities of the people but also on the proper development of the sermon, the basic needs of the people, and the competence of the preacher.

There is a place for righteous indignation in the body of the sermon and in the conclusion at times, but there is never a place for "hot" or "cold" anger against the people God has committed to our care. James Stewart's counsel is pure gold: "You will never weaken the force of your final appeal by keeping it restrained. In nine cases out of ten, quiet notes are better than crashing chords." [12] "Vision, not violence, persuades parishioners," is the way Theodore Ferris put it.[13] Most preachers learn this early in their ministry. All preachers, being human, forget it occasionally under personal and public pressure. Congre-

gations understand, forgive, and forget occasional out-
bursts; but they will not tolerate many. No sudden surge
of emotionalism, display of histrionics, or rhetoric without
substance can redeem a weak sermon, and it will dissipate
the impact of a strong one. "It is a pity," says James Black,
"if our finish should finish us. . . ." [14]

Do not re-preach the sermon in your conclusion. I have
done that, loathe to let God's people go and equally re-
luctant to let go of "my" sermon. Conclude! Sit down!
Everyone, God as well as the congregation, will be re-
lieved. Your wife and children will call you blessed. You
will likely live to preach another day. James Black cites
Oliver Wendell Holmes' description of guests who do not
know how to take their leave. "They want to be off, and
we want them to be off, but they don't know how to manage it. One would think they . . . were waiting to be
launched." That is a fair representation of the preacher
who has trouble ending his or her sermon. Black observes:
"He wants to finish . . . and you want him to finish. But
he cannot secure a decent or effective exit; so he takes
another aimless amble round the room!" [15] "Amen" is as
welcome at the end of a sermon that has gotten too long
as it is to a pastoral prayer that has informed God in detail of what he already knows.

Do not back away from a direct, vigorously spoken appeal to persons to do this or that specific work for Christ.
Convinced that the Word of the Lord always calls for a
fresh personal decision to follow Christ more courageous-
ly, honor his demands more responsibly, do his work more
urgently, and love him more selflessly, I have aimed at
getting personal decisions for Christ in every sermon I
have ever preached. Some sermons have been more effective than others, but a call for decision, implicit or explicit, has been in every sermon—at least, it has been in-

tended. The call can be direct and specific or indirect and inclusive. It is a mark of biblical preaching. Preachers who have worked responsibly and prayerfully in their study and have preached Christ persuasively in the hour of worship can appeal to the hearers' wills as well as to their intellects and emotions. Jesus said, "If any man's will is to do his will, he shall know whether the teaching is from God or whether I am speaking on my own authority" (John 7:17).

Jesus' answer to the question, "Who is my neighbor?" is the enduring story of the Good Samaritan. He ended that parable with a forthright directive: "Go and do likewise." Jesus' call to obedience is set down in four plain words, two of which are imperatives: "*Go* and *do* likewise." Jesus also declared: "He who is not with me is against me." Be specific. Be concrete. Speak God's whole counsel. Clergy, preaching on the poignant story of the woman taken in adultery, lift strongly before their congregations the glad news that God accepts us as we are, forgives us, and opens new life to us in Christ. But too many preachers, having proclaimed God's love through that event, fail to conclude the sermon with Jesus' final command to the forgiven woman: "Go and sin no more." Christian liberty is not license. Freedom without discipline ends in anarchy even as discipline without freedom ends in tyranny. The gospel offers responsible freedom through willing obedience to Christ. In Christ, demand and promise are joined as one. Our preaching must not separate what God joins together. The call for personal decision, explicit or implicit, is a mark of biblical preaching. To come face-to-face with the Lord of the Scriptures is to decide for or against him. That call is in the conclusion to every biblical sermon.

Preaching a stewardship sermon titled, "Let the Redeemed of the Lord Say So!", I concluded in this straightforward fashion.

> The church's primary need is to accept Christ as Lord. God's purposes are frustrated historically wherever his Son's authority is unrecognized, winked at, rejected. Obedience, no less than intellectual assent and trust, is an integral part of Christian Faith. "Faith" which fails to persuade its professor to acknowledge and act on Christ's orders is sentimentalism, hypocrisy, false piety— or a witches brew of all three. The Christian, abhorring cheap grace, asks "Do I acknowledge Christ as Lord of my life?" That's where stewardship begins and never ends.
>
> The questions—"Do I have the money to give?" "Does this church deserve economic support?" "Does Christ need money?"—are evasive, patronizing, and, if persisted in, damning. Mature Christians ask: "How much can I keep without stunting my growth in Christian personhood?" "How can I resist giving beyond my means in the face of a love so amazing?" "Does my giving demonstrate that Christ is the Lord of my life?"
>
> Now, let the redeemed of the Lord in this congregation say so!

Of course, the preacher's tone of voice and inflection, personal attitude toward his hearers ("your attitude is showing!"), and body language are important. This is especially true when preachers allow the Word to confront persons through them. It is especially important when they focus the call for decision in the conclusion. The human spiirt will not be coerced. Vision persuades; violence alienates. God himself respects every person's freedom to say no. He wants sons and daughters, not slaves or hired hands. His heralds respect him by respecting his people's freedom. But most preachers need to learn that confrontation (truth spoken in love) is *not* a violation of human freedom. In fact, it shows respect for it. Preachers and parishioners alike need to learn that love without truth at its center is shapeless and powerless; and that truth without love crushes or alienates the human spirt. The "religion of civility" is not biblical Christianity. There is too much at stake to be "polite."

Do not rely on the momentum of a well-prepared, content-filled sermon preached in the uplifting spirit of worship to provide an effective conclusion on the spot. I tried that for years. My sermons built "to a series of conclusions which never concluded!"[16] An examination of my sermon files for the first fifteen years reveals carefully written sermons *without* written conclusions. Only rarely in those years can I find a single sentence suggesting a possible conclusion. My problem was sloth. Having worked diligently on the body of the sermon, its introduction, and its title, I lacked the discipline to finish properly what I had begun seriously and worked on arduously and prayerfully. One day, I faced my sloth by an act of will and have written out most of my conclusions ever since. Sloth, a human disease, is hard to cure. Like malaria, it lingers on, causing trouble periodically in some area of our full ministry.

While I do not agree with those who insist that the conclusion is the most crucial two minutes in the sermon, I grant readily that it is crucial to effective preaching. But all three parts of the sermon—introduction, body, conclusion—together with the title and the act of proclamation add up to effective or ineffective preaching. No part of the sermon or any aspect of the act of preaching can be treated casually without lessening the impact of the message.

A well-constructed sermon rooted in the Word carries its own conclusion. If you cannot get hold of it in writing the sermon, you should reexamine the sermon for biblical and theological soundness, inner logic, structural balance, unity, symmetry, and common sense—or ask whether you are trying to devise a conclusion that will do in two minutes what it requires a life-time of ministry to do. The Holy Spirit works in spite of our poor efforts. One need not despair. But his work is hindered by our slovenly efforts. One should not presume. Ideally, each member in the congregation, in the course of the sermon and especially in its concluding moments, should feel that the preacher is speaking directly to him or her.

Charles H. Spurgeon closed each sermon, *having planned his conclusion with that end in view,* to bring God's truth home to the mind and heart and will of *one* person. Spurgeon, speaking to six thousand persons every Sunday, came through as one preaching person-to-person. Harry Emerson Fosdick was fond of saying in his sermons, "Perhaps I speak to one person here today who needs this message." James Stewart did that, too. The personal note rings out in all effective biblical preaching even as it does in the Lord's Supper—"for you." If preachers fail to sound this note, they deny their hearers the full splendor and power of the gospel. We preachers are engaged in serious work: "Knowing therefore the fear of the Lord, we persuade men" (2 Cor. 5:1). Undeserving beneficiaries of God's mercy, we preachers, like our parishioners, are under God's judgment.

A final word on conclusions. Do not be like Pharaoh in your pulpit each Sunday forcing God to cry out against you: "Let my people go." End with the same sense of urgency that the Word engenders throughout the sermon. Say what God commissioned you to say, say it as well as you can, and be done with it. "When the moment of insight has come . . . stop talking. When the Word has happened there is nothing to do but to enter into it, to share it in prayer, in song, and in quietly being together." [17]

A TITLE FOR THE SERMON

The most effective sermon saddled with a carelessly devised title, or denied one, will lose some of its appeal before it is preached and part of its impact after it has been preached. A sermon that opens hearts and minds to Christ deserves a fitting title. The resurrected Christ, King of kings and Lord of lords, ought to be announced properly every Sunday. A solid content sermon, carefully structured, gracefully worded, and persuasively preached deserves a title for *invitation* and for *remembrance*. A proper title is integral to a sermon's content, a strand in the Christian education of the congregation in their preparing to hear it and in their remembrance of it, and to the preacher's knowing what he or she intends to say.

To be sure, titling sermons poses problems. The "working title" may be integral to the sermon in the preacher's mind, but its phrasing must make the sermon content clear to the hearers' minds. Examine each title critically against the backdrop of the different social and racial groups in your congregation. In our era, thousands of words have two or three or more meanings for people in different cultural strata. Some of those meanings obscure or make absurd what you intend to say. See to it that the title says to others what you intend to preach about. Work to make it speak with integrity to as many unchurched people as possible. Do not try to be clever.

Keep alert also to the effect of the title in relation to the preacher's name when the two appear together. Ralph Sockman liked to tell of the week in Christ Church, New York City, when the church's outdoor bulletin board carried his Sunday sermon subject, "Christ's Chief Enemy," and beneath his title in small letters, "Doctor Sockman will preach." At one time or other, every preacher is Christ's chief enemy, but there is no sense in publishing the fact. If the church uses printed bulletins which carry the titles of hymns, the preacher will be alert to how the sermon title meshes with the titles of the pre-sermon and recessional hymns. If you have preached a rousing sermon on Paul's "I have run a good race . . . ," you will not choose to close the service with the hymn, "O, Day of Rest and Gladness"! Correlation between hymn content and sermon content is even more crucial. The worship service should be of a piece.

So, each sermon title will fit the particular sermon it announces. It will be integral to the sermon, descriptive of its purpose, and relevant to the hearers' life situations. The sermon is not ready to be preached until the minister gets hold of its indigenous title. An honest, attractive title prods people to prepare for a sermon; it also helps them to remember a particular sermon. Who can forget Clarence Edward McCartney's sermon on the end of opportunity, "Come Before Winter," or Arthur John Gossip's sermon on God's sustaining power, "When Life Tumbles In, What Then?"

But a good introduction, a solid conclusion, and an attractive title cannot save a poorly constructed sermon that lacks content and is preached without conviction. We shall attempt to bring all this together in the next chapter which focuses on the act of preaching.

10 The Word of God and the Preacher's Words

The Word dwelled with God, and what God was, the Word was. The Word, then, was with God at the beginning . . . no single thing was created without him. . . . So the Word became flesh . . . and we saw his glory.

—John 1:1-2 and 14 (NEB)

The being of man is founded in language.

—Martin Heidegger

PART OF THE CULTURAL PROBLEM that biblical preachers face is in their primary tools—words. These tools are hard to handle. They require understanding and skill. Words mean different things to different people at different times. They always have. Presently, however, the task of using words to communicate reality is especially difficult because our language has been badly debased. It is used to manipulate, stimulate, entice, intimidate, and deceive. It is used thoughtlessly. It is over-used compulsively. From transistor and auto radios, motion pictures, TV, newspapers, ecclesiastical magazines, secular magazines, specialists' journals, and pulpits tidal waves of carelessly used and debased words engulf us. A word means what a huckster

160

or politician or casual lover or ethnic group or specialist
says it means.[1]

But God's heralds are unique. They are appointed to
employ human words to communicate his Word to persons living in a world of illusions created by the words
of ignorant, confused, devious people, themselves among
them. One reason why biblical preaching is crucial in any
age is that it enables us to discern and cope with reality.
But if the preacher does not believe that God's Word has
the power to liberate responsive persons, or believing it,
lacks confidence in the human activity of preaching, he or
she will not use human words effectively in proclaiming
God's good news in Christ.

Words are deeds. That is uniquely true when they
communicate the mighty acts of God: his liberation of
the Hebrews from bondage; his testing and shaping of
a "chosen" people whose remembered experience of his
generous dealings provided part of the historical context
for Jesus' full revelation of his Father's love; and his advent into history in the person of Jesus of Nazareth. Human words—chosen precisely, arranged to reveal God
anew (the form of the sermon), and spoken from personal
conviction—are the vehicles for God's living Word in
biblical preaching. God, speaking through the words and
person of his messengers, acts anew in human history.
Luther, like Paul before him and Pannenberg after him,
pointed out that history makes sense because of God's
past, present, and future action in it. History is to be interpreted by that ongoing revelation, and by personal experience. Both tasks are large strands in every Christian
preacher's vocation. Human language is the means whereby God *has* spoken and *continues* to speak his Word to
men and women. Consequently, the preacher's words are

crucial. They reveal God in his grace and glory or obscure him from view.

Human words are also expressions and extensions of our being. Our being is, as Heidegger averred, "founded in language." Language provides the symbols we use to perceive, understand, and communicate reality. Our words hide, caricature, or reveal who we are and what we are doing in this world. They are the major means through which we discern and respond to reality or embrace illusions. What is open and what is concealed can be expressed in words. In Shakespeare's *Othello,* Iago, envying the Moor's goodness and Desdemona's love for him, undermines their beautiful relationship by speaking dishonest words which arouse Othello's jealousy. Words are also deeds. When Franklin Roosevelt assured the American people in 1933 that "the only thing we have to fear is fear itself," he steadied millions of frightened people. When Winston Churchill delivered his "blood, sweat, and tears" challenge to the joint Houses of Parliament in late May, 1940, he rallied a disheartened nation to its "finest hour." It is equally true that Hitler and his amoral wordsmith, Joseph Goebbels—employing human language and capitalizing on Germany's historical situation—persuaded and bullied Nazi Germany and its satellite states to commit the most hideous acts of genocide in human history.

Words are deeds for good or evil in the public arena. Words are deeds of hurt or healing in intimate relationships. It is said that a picture is worth a thousand words. That is not true. Every deaf person knows that. Turn the sound off on a TV presentation of the news or a political debate, and you soon lose interest. The commonest complaint in marriage counseling is double-barreled: "He (she) doesn't communicate; and she (he) doesn't really hear what I say." Words are deeds in the family, the

marketplace, the political arena, and the church. Chosen
precisely and linked together to form sound structures
for communicating God's truth, words reveal reality. If
Jesus had gone about demonstrating the person of God
without describing God as he is, we mortals would not
know God at all. If he had gone directly to Calvary without a word, we would not know what he has done for us
or what he expects of us. No picture or painting can
match the images conjured in the human mind by Jesus'
parables. The words he spoke were so much a part of
his daily deeds, revelatory of his person, that the Christian community identified him as *the* Word (John 1:1-14).

Biblical preachers love words because they love God's
Word. They work hard at putting words together leanly
to communicate directly and clearly to people what the
Spirit has persuaded them to say for God. They use words
honestly, as a friend speaks them; skillfully, as the novelist
employs them; insightfully, as the poet chooses them;
carefully, as the advocate speaks them; clear-headedly, as
the teacher uses them; and graciously, as the lover whis-
pers them to his or her beloved. Responsible preachers
never forget that "somebody out there is listening." [2]

But in this electronic age, "the human sensorium," as
Walter Ong calls our total perceptual apparatus, is radically different from people's perceptual capabilities in the
first Christian century or in the Middle Ages or in 1950
for that matter. It is the preacher's responsibility to proclaim God's changeless truth in the changing images of
a changing culture and in the idiom of the people. The
biblical preacher—like the prophets, Jesus, the twelve
apostles, and Paul—uses secular language. This continuing
burden in preaching would crush preachers except that
the strong Word they proclaim is the sustaining Word
that enables them to proclaim it. Here, as everywhere,

God's grace abounds. Paul, confronting the opinionated band of Christians at Corinth, asks bitingly: "What do you possess that has not been given you? And if it was given you, why do you boast as if it had been gained, not given?" (2 Cor. 4:7). Christ enables whom he calls.

Biblical preachers mean what they say; they speak with conviction. They also say simply and directly what they mean; they speak with clarity. They address the whole "human sensorium" in concrete images that are indigenous to their culture. Paul did that magnificently. Jesus did it perfectly. Biblical sermons preached with conviction and clarity and imagination become the powerful human means whereby the Spirit calls, enlightens, and refashions responsive persons in Christ's likeness. They also have an impact on society.[3] "See, I have set my words in your mouth . . . to destroy and to overthrow, to build and to plant" (Jer. 1:10).

How one puts words together, E. B. White observes, is one's unique style.[4] In the case of biblical preaching, however, it is more than the preacher's style. It is a revelation of his or her person as well as God's Word. The sermon proclaimed becomes the preacher's identified action with the Word itself. Each sermon is not only an intrinsic communication of God's truth as objective reality, as James Rees observes, but also the sharing of what has come alive in the person of the preacher. Choosing the right words and putting them together honestly and insightfully and persuasively is basic in biblical preaching.

Abraham Lincoln could have phrased his Gettysburg Address in these words: "Eighty-seven years ago our ancestors established a Republic in the middle of North America so that they could guarantee for themselves civil liberties which had been denied them in Europe, and, through a sane political framework, fashion an orderly society. . . ." If President Lincoln had written those words, his judgment that "the world will little note nor long remember what we say here . . ." would have been accurate!

Lincoln's masterful "Four-score and seven years ago . . ." address was not dashed off on the back of an envelope on the train from Washington to Gettysburg on 21 November, 1863. Three drafts of the "Gettysburg Address" are extant. Lincoln began writing it months before he delivered it. Its content and style were in the making when Lincoln debated Douglas for the Illinois senatorship in 1858. They were evident in his campaign speech at Cooper Union in 1860. One could also trace the lineage of Lincoln's famous address back to his boyhood reading of Parson Weem's *Life of Washington* for its political idealism and to his study of the King James' Bible for its cadenced style. Greater yet than Lincoln's brief address at Gettysburg is his Second Inaugural Address. Its closing paragraph, a single sentence of seventy-two words, was prophetic and is sublime: "With malice toward none, with charity for all, with firmness in the right as God gives us to see the right. . . ." That is the way the English language is intended to be used. Mr. Lincoln used words to serve this Republic. Biblical preachers use words to serve the kingdom of God.

Choosing the right words and putting them together simply, clearly, and imaginatively to communicate reality is demanding work. Examine Paul's description of Christian love in the thirteenth chapter of I Corinthians. Those familiar words, arranged with grace and logic, appeal to the mind, heart, and will; they capture the human imagination. That is so because of the content. It is also true because of the form and style. Tamper with the structure, form, and style of any great literary work—Tolstoy's *War and Peace,* for example—and its meaning is diminished, distorted, or lost. Preachers need to remind themselves that "forms of words are expressions of the ceaseless creative activity of God without whom no words can be made and used in meaningful conjunction." [5] Language is God's unique gift to human creatures. It is also a field for his continuing acts of creation and redemption. [5]

But preachers need not get compulsive about ferreting out the right words, endlessly rearranging and pruning their written material. The sermon is written to be *proclaimed* in the hour of worship. There the Spirit gives the *prepared* preacher his words so that God himself is present in the proclamation. This is not to suggest that every parishioner will hear God's Word, or do it. No matter how clearly preachers say what they mean and how earnestly they mean what they say and how relevant their images and concepts of Christ and his way of life are, some people in their congregations will not understand what they say, or understanding it, will not accept and do it. But the biblical preacher does not excuse careless or indifferent preaching or sporadic pastoral work on the ground that some people appear to prefer darkness to light. The Spirit of God can get through psychic barriers that psychiatrists and other humans cannot penetrate. Jesus said to the hard-bitten, wealthy tax collector, Zacchaeus, "I shall have dinner with you tonight." No one had spoken previously to that man's awful loneliness! It is not the preacher's business to determine whose heart is hardened against God. It is his or her business to preach the life-giving Word to a dying people in the most effective human words he or she can devise. Biblical preaching is itself an act of faith in the power of God's Word to penetrate the barriers erected by sin.

A few earnest preachers get so preoccupied with words

and structure and style that they lose sight of the Word
and the purpose of the sermon. It is critical in effective
preaching to get the right words, but it is crucial in biblical preaching to discern and proclaim the Word. Since
the sermon is communicated by a person to persons-in-
community, prepared preachers can, in extempore preaching, get away with a few dangling participles, a free-
floating pronoun or two, an infelicitous phrase, even an
unfinished sentence here and there. The spoken word is
less precise than the written word. And the biblical
preacher is known and valued for more than his or her
skill with words. "It is his holding fast to sound doctrine
that makes his skill with words possible and the patterns
he weaves with them meaningful." [7] Biblical content, cultural relevance, and personal conviction, as well as sermon structure and style, are inseparable in biblical preaching. The substantive and the methodological come together in the *effective* proclamation of gospel truth.

Can God be patient then with preachers who, because
of sloth, will not dig out the right words and labor into
the night and get up early in the morning to put the right
words together to communicate his Word persuasively?
He deserves our best work with words, because our parishioners need our best words to perceive and understand
God's life-giving Word. The Polish-English novelist, Joseph Conrad, author of those magnificent sea stories,
cried: "Give me the right word and the right accent and
I will move the world." The Evangelist John said, "In the
beginning was the Word . . ." Getting that Word into
intelligible human words and proclaiming it with interest
and conviction to persons-in-community is biblical preaching.

Several observations on the *act* of preaching may be
helpful.

First, each preacher is a distinct and unique person. Individuality is the "touch of spice"[8] each human being brings to his or her sermon, and whole ministry for that matter. The carefully prepared biblical sermon is, when preached, Christ appealing by a particular preacher whom he has chosen and called to do his work. The twelve disciples were individuals. The four evangelists were distinctively different persons. It is dangerous to dwell too much on the *techniques* of the act of preaching. Each preacher should be allowed to develop his or her own style. God did not give Paul gifts that made him an "attractive" speaker.[9] He gave Paul a message, a personal faith, fierce determination, and intellectual abilities that enabled him to plant the Word in the hearts and minds of persons around the Mediterranean world. Dwight L. Moody fractured the King's English, but his preaching opened new life to tens of thousands. Charles H. Spurgeon was often pedestrian, but he never slandered the grace of God in his own heart. A. J. Gossip could get so enmeshed in classical quotations and allusions as to exasperate his hearers (and readers), but his knowledge of and commitment to God's Word always broke through. Second only to the preacher's personal call is his or her providential call (natural endowments, social grace, presence). We should not tamper with or repress these providential gifts; they can be profitable to the gospel.

All biblical preachers have personal limitations. Moses stuttered. Elijah got depressed. Jeremiah complained. Peter broke down under pressure. Other heroes of the faith had their shortcomings, too. Protestants wish avidly that Luther had been gracious with Erasmus, compassionate toward the peasants, open to the Jews, and less deferential to secular rulers. They also wish that Calvin had not focused so exclusively on the sovereignty of God and had not approved the execution of Michael Servetus. Roman Catholics, and Protestants, too, wish that Thomas Aquinas had been less Aristotelian and more Christian in his *Summa* and that Pope Pius XII had spoken out boldly against the Nazi policy of genocide against the Jews. Yet God used these contentious, brilliant, violent, arrogant, cautious, disintegrating earthen vessels to carry his treasure to millions of spiritually impoverished people. Leslie J. Tizard recalls what every preacher learns: "It is a comforting, yet humbling thought that God sometimes uses us when we are at our worst to make us helpful to others. I cannot tell how it happens, but I know it does. If it were not so, I should more often be in despair." [10] So would we all! But we preachers dare not presume on God's grace; he expects us to do our best work at all times. There is joy as well as anguish in biblical preaching, for it *is* hard work to move from inspiration and conception to effective writing and persuasive proclamation.

Second, stop thinking and talking about the *delivery* of sermons. Mail, drug prescriptions, lectures, and babies are delivered. Sermons are proclaimed; they are not delivered. In the fullness of time, God did not deliver his message; he came himself in the person of his Son. Neither God nor his good news can be packaged or gift-wrapped for delivery. Consequently, biblical preaching is emotionally exhausting work as well as demanding intellectual work. The preacher is *used* by God's Spirit; message and messenger become one. Dick Sheppard preached himself to death in London after World War I. Kaj Munk, Bonhoeffer, and King paid the last full measure of devotion to bring God's Word to persons through their persons. The rest of us who preach God's truth in concrete contemporary images (secular language) so that people decide for or against Christ, experience indifference, anger, hostility, derision, and rejection as well as interest, acceptance, and love. Such preaching is exhausting as well as exhilarating, for we preachers *are* identified with the message as well as the bearers of it. Biblical preaching is intellectually taxing, emotionally draining, volitionally enervating. Biblical sermons are proclaimed with "fear and trembling." They are not delivered like mail or recited as a gifted child recites "Hiawatha"!

The *third* observation about the *act* of preaching centers on every preacher's "Hamlet question": to use or not to use a full manuscript in the pulpit. Some preachers never resolve this question cleanly in a lifetime of preaching. Their work and their people suffer for this indecision. To be effective, each preacher must decide this matter firmly one way or the other and then work diligently to become accomplished in preaching *with* or *without* a manuscript. Preaching carefully prepared sermons without a manuscript or notes adds to the burden of preaching. In my experience, it has never gotten lighter.

On the other hand, preaching well from a full manuscript is extremely difficult. Since the sermon cannot be "delivered" like a lecture or read like an essay, the manuscript must be used so skillfully that God's message comes through the preacher's person to persons in the congregation in spite of it. The decision one makes about the sermon manuscript will affect his or her preaching style. Paul Scherer quotes a Scottish woman's pertinent and impertinent criticisms of a sermon she had heard: "It was read, it was no' read well, it was no' worth reading." He goes on to say, "Reading is far too impersonal a method for the pulpit." [11] But Peter Marshall, Harry Emerson Fosdick, and Phillips Brooks did not find it so. They were effective proclaimers of God's Word. *There is no fixed rule.*

A few preachers choose to memorize their sermons verbatim. Clarence Edward McCartney crowded First Presbyterian Church in downtown Pittsburgh Sunday mornings, evenings, and Wednesday and Thursday noons for thirty years, circa 1925-1955. He wrote every sermon fully. He memorized every word of every manuscript, preaching four times a week. I stand in awe of such preaching. I cannot quote verbatim a single stanza from the most familiar hymn! Paul Scherer told the divinity students at Yale in 1944 that two or three hours with his fully written manuscript on a Saturday afternoon allowed him to do it "letter perfect" on Sunday.[12]

I do not have that faculty either. I recall material in context. What I have worked through carefully and written out precisely remains mine in *substance* and comes to mind readily in the act of extempore preaching. This kind of preaching allows the preacher to *speak* simply and directly. It sets him or her free to shorten or lengthen an introduction and/or conclusion on the spot. It opens the door to spontaneous humor which can ease heavy content or underscore a point. For one who preaches the same sermon at two or three Sunday services, it allows him or her to sharpen the clarity and correct the balance of the sermon from one service to the next. Best of all, preaching without manuscript or notes allows for eye contact. But it does play havoc with one's literary style, if that really matters.

Preaching is visual-aural. If you decide to use a manuscript, *learn to read* so well that it is not a barrier in the visual-aural encounter of preaching. Write out your sermon carefully; strip it of verbiage; check it critically on purpose, structure, movement, and style; study it for several hours; open yourself to the Spirit's presence and then proclaim the glad, good news with or without the manuscript. Go tell the people what God has done in Christ for others, and for you, and what he wants to do for them, and can, and will, when they respond to him in faith. *Tell the Story* the best way *you* can!

The *fourth* observation about the act of preaching centers on dialog. Biblical preaching is by its nature dialogical; it creates public dialog. Authentic dialog is not contrived. First, the Holy Spirit, working mediately through the Word, initiates the dialog and keeps it alive. What God says to us is a matter of life or death. When the preacher gets this across in the images and idioms of the people, he or she is preaching dialogically. Second, the human spirit yearns for fellowship with God, to tell him of hurt and accept healing, to confess rebellion and experience reconciliation, to speak of failures and gain strength (comfort) from his power. People caught up in God's Word engage spontaneously in God-talk (theology) with others. Third, faithful pastoral work, insights from biblical study, cultural reading, and responsible citizenship make the preacher sensitive to and concerned for *all* people as human beings in need of liberation. Biblical preaching anticipates and identifies these unvoiced human needs. The Holy Spirit, working mediately through the Word in the human activity of preaching, divides a crowd into individuals. Dialog results.

There is urgent need for dialog in our congregations, between Christians of one tradition and other traditions, between Christians and scientists and philosophers, business people and political leaders, and . . . the whole world. Biblical preaching and evangelical teaching stimulate and foster dialog between pulpit and pew and, in time, between pew and marketplace, laboratory, academia—all segments of society.[13] The Christian pulpit is the place for heralding God's good news and instructing people in the truth about him, themselves, and society; for helping them to recognize and experience God's presence and power; and for motivating them to work for a just society here and now. Biblical preaching stirs dialog and deeds; polite homilies and "dialog sermons" do not. When a congregation and their preacher can say of the formal preaching in their hour of worship, "thus saith the Lord," both congregation and pastor will be motivated and equipped to get into serious dialog with the world—to care for the lonely, the dispossessed, the oppressed, the hungry, the under-loved, and the lost here and now.

Finally, biblical preachers will review and reflect on these aspects of preaching.

Body language—tone of voice, flash of eye, turn of lip, open hand, clenched fist, accusing finger—is part of biblical preaching. Walter Ong reminds us that one communicates "with his whole body. . . ." [14] That should be obvious. It is not, however, to some formally educated persons. They are too cerebral. They repress honest emotion. Be natural in speech, movement, and manner. If a personal mannerism is not distracting to the congregation and you have not fabricated it or copied it from another preacher, continue to use it. It is the human ego rather than a particular mannerism that blocks the Word in preaching.

Do not say anything from the pulpit that you would not say person-to-person anywhere in the parish, community, or denomination. And for the sake of your own credibility and for the good of your people, do say anywhere and everywhere what you say from your pulpit. I am not suggesting that one should act out the preaching ministry all week. That would guarantee the loss of mate, children, and parishioners in short order! I am saying that the person who preaches for twenty-five minutes each Sunday morning in a particular congregation must come through in what he or she says and how he or she acts then exactly as he or she comes through during the other one-hundred-sixty-seven-and-a-half hours of the week. The preacher is not a stage or TV actor with a role to play. The preacher is a human steward of the mysteries of God made known in Christ. A preaching self and a pastoral self, a social self and a family self produce a "ministerial schizophrenia" that robs the preacher of his or her credibility, unsettles one's family, divides the congregation. Every preacher is a human being called first to be a Christian and thereafter to be a pastor who is, in turn, called through the church to serve a particular congregation. You are the person God created, Christ redeemed, and his Spirit uses. Be your redeemed self everytime, in and outside the pulpit. It is the best "role" you will ever get. It is pure gift. Use it to God's glory!

You will be influenced, of course, by the work and witness of other preachers in your sermon preparation and in the act of preaching. You will prime your pump from the clear-headed thinking of others—theologians, biblical scholars, ethicists, preachers, novelists, poets, historians, biographers, philosophers, political leaders, parishioners—but you will not steal another preacher's sermon. You will not wittingly claim another person's thought or experience as your own. Some ministers who speak from their pulpits against corporate theft in Detroit and Pittsburgh, Capetown and Tokyo, have themselves engaged in serious theft that same week. Let it be said strongly: the biblical preacher does not steal other preacher's sermons or subscribe to a "sermon service" to *parrot* what he or she buys

there. One does not pass off another person's experience
as his own. One does not emulate deliberately another
preacher's literary or preaching style. One does not copy
another preacher's natural mannerisms. Theft undoes
many promising preachers of the Word.

What about reading printed sermons? Do it. Read them
devotionally. A. J. Gossip has been my private chaplain
for three decades. Read them critically. Stewart and Fosdick, Scherer and Ferris, David Roberts and Frederick
Buechner have been my models for style, clarity and interest. Study printed sermons from Chrysostom to Billy
Graham. The solid witness of our colleagues in the Faith
does more than prime our pumps. It puts new heart in
our preaching. It prods us to do our best work. It also
teaches us that *our* preaching is not extraordinary and
that many preachers have been and are extraordinarily
effective in the congregations God called them to serve.
The study of printed sermons is humbling and uplifting
as well as enlightening, corrective, and supportive.

One thing more. Do not refer to your travels in your
sermons. In this jet age, thousands of preachers have traveled to all parts of the world to preach, lecture, study,
and visit. "The Last Time I Saw Paris" can be set to music, but references to personal travels do not enhance
one's sermons. If you have been enriched by travel, let it
show in the quality of your preaching. Confine the facts
to your speaker's vita! The same counsel holds for the
books one reads, the stimulating persons one meets, the
rich experiences one is privileged to have. Biblical preaching is a solid witness to the Word, not a travelog, a pale
copy of the Book Review section of the *New York Times,*
or a page from *Who's Who in America.* Petty minds gossip about other people. Pedestrian minds discuss where
they have been, who they know, and the books they have

read. Maturing minds wrestle with the meaning of events, ideas, concepts, human nature, and the intentions of God-in-Christ in their unflagging quest for truth-reality.

Biblical preaching is Christ appealing by you. It is his story and the church's story before it is your story, but there is that point when it becomes *your* story. What Christopher Morley said about a good book can be said about a good sermon: "It ought to come like Eve from somewhere near the third rib; there ought to be a heart beating in it." [15] There will be a growing mind and committed will in it too. Biblical preachers love the Lord their God with all their heart and mind and will, and other people as they love themselves.

To be a biblical preacher, then, is to rely on God. That is the heart of it: God-reliance, not self-reliance. Preaching, like all Christian life and witness, is not a human achievement but a gift from God. We are not princes and princesses of the pulpit but servants of the Word. We are not "professionals" who control human situations but heralds of the Word that accomplishes God's purposes. We have nothing that God has not given us and whatever goodness there is in us is by his grace. This biblical concept of humility and trust is hard to grasp. It is even harder to live by. We are new creatures in Christ, but we are still creatures. Our willfulness keeps surging to the fore. We want to make it on our own. Luther, in his sermon, "On the Sum of the Christian Life," confessed:

> Let anybody try this (dependence on God's grace) and he will see and experience how exceedingly hard and bitter a thing it is for a man, who all his life has been mired in his work righteousness, to pull himself out of it and with all his heart rise up through faith in this one Mediator. I myself have now been preaching and cultivating it through reading and writing for almost twenty

years and still I feel the old clinging dirt of wanting to deal so with God that I may contribute something, so that he will have to give me his grace in exchange for my holiness. And still I cannot get it into my head that I should surrender myself completely to sheer grace; yet this is what I should and must do.[16]

So must we all if we are to preach biblically!

Worship and witness are inseparable. Biblical preaching is at the center of both. It has been from the beginning. It must be again, if the world is to listen to the church.

Now, Finally

It is one thing to see the land of peace from a
wooded ridge . . . and another to tread the road
that leads to it.

—St. Augustine, *Confessions,* VII, 21

BIBLICAL PREACHERS ARE SERVANTS OF THE WORD;
they are not galley slaves. They are under-
shepherds, not sheep dogs. As each person is
the unique handiwork of God the Creator and
has his or her own "touch of spice," so each Christian
person is the unique handiwork of the Holy Spirit, a new
creature in Christ, having in him or her a measure of
Christ's own mind. Called to be co-laborers with God's
Son and co-heirs with him, biblical preachers place their
confidence in God's Word *and* in the human activity of
proclaiming it. They have discovered firsthand that God's
Spirit works mediately through his Word. They know
that any lack of confidence in either the Word or the
human activity of preaching robs the preacher of God's
power, delimits the congregation's understanding of
Christ, and diminishes their witness and service in the
world.

Biblical preachers know that they stumble more than
they stride, yet they speak of their vocation to preach as

urgently as the actress, Julie Harris, spoke of her vocation
to act: "It is my life!" But there is another dimension, a
dark dimension, to the biblical preacher's call: "Woe is
me if I preach not God's glorious gospel." Every preacher
is haunted by that reality. God is not mocked. His righteousness as well as his mercy covers all that he creates
and, in Christ, re-creates. It is an awesome experience to
fall into the hands of the gracious God, the Father of our
Lord, Jesus Christ. Every biblical preacher's call is tarnished, sometimes badly, but by God's grace the sheer
wonder of it is there to the end.

Preaching God's searing-healing Word is gruelling work.
It always has been. It was demanding work to preach
God's Word effectively against the glory that was Greece
and the grandeur and decadence that was Rome. It was
frustrating work to preach in the world that produced the
Gothic cathedrals and the *Canterbury Tales.* It was difficult work to preach in the Age of Rationalism with Voltaire to point up the foibles of the institutional church. It
was exhausting work to preach in poverty-ridden eigh-
teenth-century London. It was dangerous work to preach
on the American frontier. It was costly work to preach
God's Word concretely and specifically in America during
the turgid 1950s, the turbulent 1960s, and the narcissistic
1970s, and to preach it on the mission fields after World
War II when new nations in Africa and Asia were struggling to be born. It will be even more demanding, I judge,
to preach God's Word responsibly in the changing cultures
and unstable political communities of this world during
the last two decades of the twentieth century and in the
early decades of the 21st century.

But Paul's appraisal of the preaching office (task, function) remains valid: Preach the Word in season and out
of season; it is the power of God to those who believe.

Jesus—who came preaching, "The kingdom of God is at hand. Repent! Believe!"—is our model and enabler in this Christian work. The church's discovery of the secret of being born again generation after generation is bound inextricably with the effective proclamation of the whole counsel of God. That was so in the first generation of Christians. It is true in this generation. It will be true in the next . . . and the next . . . until Christ comes again in all his power and glory.

To be entrusted by God with his gospel, as every Christian is, makes royalty of his truth-bearers. As there is no other name in heaven or earth save that of Jesus, so there is no vocation that is higher, no task more significant, no work more enduring than to preach Christ crucified, raised from the dead, gloriously alive in a dying world, willing and able to make us conquerors, too! There is no better news than that. But too often

> . . . it is the preacher who as steward of the wildest mystery of them all is the one who hangs back, prudent, cautious, hopelessly mature and wise to the last, when no less than St. Paul tells us to be fools for Christ's sake. . . .[1]

Biblical preachers—remembering the resurrected Christ's thrice-repeated question to Simon Peter after that brash man's mean denials, "Do you love me?" and realizing that their own love for Christ moves them to preach even as his love calls them to and sustains them in that work—plead with their people, "Let your religion be less of a theory and more of a love affair."[2] Ah, yes! A love affair with God, his people, your self, and his world; for love, stronger than sin and death, endures forever. The empty cross is God's affirmation of that.

"Mortal man, stand up, I want to talk to you. . . .
Mortal man, I am sending you to the people. . . ."
(Ezek. 2:1 and 3 GNB)

"Woe to me if I do not preach the gospel"
(1 Cor. 9:16 RSV)

"Simon, son of John, do you love me? . . . Take care of my
sheep"
(John 21:15-19 GNB)

"Yes indeed! I am coming soon!"
(Rev. 22:20a GNB)

"So be it. Come, Lord Jesus!"
(Rev. 22:20b GNB)

Notes

PREFACE

1. For a first-hand report, see Wallace E. Fisher, *From Tradition to Mission* (Nashville: Abingdon, 1965); Apex Paperback, 1974.
2. See Letty Russel's sermon, "The Impossible Possibility" (Isa. 52:13-15; Mk. 10:35-45), Helen Gray Crotwell, ed., *Women and the Word: Sermons* (Philadelphia: Fortress, 1978) 86-91.

INTRODUCTION

1. See Steven Weinberg, *The First Three Minutes: A Modern View of the Origin of the Universe* (New York: Basic Books, 1977), and John V. Taylor, *The Go-Between God; The Holy Spirit and the Christian Mission* (Philadelphia: Fortress, 1973). See also Preston Cloud, *Cosmos, Earth, and Man: A Short History of the Universe* (New Haven: Yale University Press, 1978), J. N. Kildahl, *The Holy Spirit and Our Faith* (Minneapolis: Augsburg, 1960), and Paul Davies, *The Runaway Universe* (New York: Harper & Row, 1978).
2. Edmund Steimle, quoted in Charles L. Rice, *Interpretation and Imagination: The Preacher and Contemporary Literature* (Philadelphia: Fortress, 1970) 2.
3. Rice, *Interpretation and Imagination,* 45.
4. Gustaf Wingren, *Gospel and Church* (Philadelphia: Fortress, 1964), Part II, Chapter 1.
5. George S. Hendry, *The Holy Spirit in Christian Theology* (Philadelphia: Westminster, 1957) 73-74.
6. See Yngve Brilioth, *A Brief History of Preaching* (Philadelphia: Fortress, 1965), trans., by Karl E. Mattson.
7. Herbert H. Farmer, *The Servant of the Word* (New York: Scribner, 1942), 18. Paperback, Fortress, 1968.

8. Reinhold Niebuhr, *The Irony of History* (New York: Scribner, 1967), p. 183.
9. See Barbara Ward and Rene Dubos, *Only One Earth: The Care and Maintenance of a Small Planet* (New York: Norton, 1972), and John R. Hadd, *The Direct Connection: Rescue From Onrushing Global Catastrophe* (New York: Vantage, 1978).

1. PREACHING, THE WORLD, AND THE CHURCH

1. C. E. Black, *The Dynamics of Modernization* (New York: Harper Torchbook, 1967), p. 4.
2. Robert H. Lifton, *Boundaries: Psychological Man in Revolution* (New York: Vintage, 1970), especially 35-60. See also Paul C. Vitz, *Psychology as Religion: The Cult of Self-Worship* (Grand Rapids: Eerdmans, 1977), and Christopher Lasch, *The Culture of Narcissism: American Life in an Age of Diminishing Expectations* (New York: Norton, 1978).
3. Peter Berger, *A Rumor of Angels* (Garden City, New York: Doubleday, 1969) 7. While some Americans turn to cults and the occult, sometimes with catastrophic consequences, the majority remain earth-bound, in bondage to a material way of looking at life.
4. Nils Alstrup Dahl, *Jesus in the Memory of the Early Church* (Minneapolis: Augsburg, 1976), Chapter 8, observes that "the rediscovery of the importance of eschatology within the New Testament has been one of the most outstanding achievements of historical theology," 120.
5. Rudolf Bultmann made this his life's work. Tens of thousands of clergy are indebted to him for prodding them to face the challenge that the historical Jesus presents to every age. The fundamental criticism of Bultmann is, in my judgment, his separation of the kerygma from history. Any serious study of the "historical Jesus" ought to begin, I think, with Bultmann's *Jesus and the Word* (New York: Scribner, 1958).
6. Jacques Barzun, *Clio and the Doctors: Psycho-History, Quanto-History, and History* (Chicago: University of Chicago Press, 1974) 3.
7. See Philip Slater, *The Pursuit of Loneliness: American Culture at the Breaking Point* (Boston: Beacon, 1970) for a philosopher's in-depth appraisal.
8. Christopher Lasch, *The Culture of Narcissism*, Preface, 18. See also Andrew Hacker, *The End of the American Era* (New York: Atheneum, 1970), especially Chapter 2, "Two Hundred

Million Egos," 9-37; and Chapter 7, "Ideology and Self-Indulgence," 148-157; and Frederick S. Perls, *In and Out of the Garbage Pail* (New York: Bantam, 1972—tenth printing, October, 1977).

9. For example, Paul S. Minear's opening sentence in his review of F. F. Bruce's, *Paul: Apostle of the Heart Set Free:* "In these days of specialized knowledge, it is rare that a single scholar attempts in a single volume to cope with the vast proliferation of studies of Paul's life and times, his letters and his thought." *(Theology Today,* vol. 35, no. 3, October, 1978.)

10. See B. F. Skinner, *Beyond Behavior* (New York: Harper & Row, 1958). See also Gore Vidal, *Kalki* (New York: Random House, 1978) for a contemporary novel like *1984* and *Brave New World;* and Herbert Hendin, *The Age of Sensation* (New York: Norton, 1975) for a psychological study of personal emotional conflicts induced by our culture. Eric Fromm, more than others, made our generation aware of culture's impact on human values and behavior.

11. Gabriel Vahanian, *God and Utopia: The Church in a Technological Civilization* (New York: Seabury, 1977) 1-20ff.

12. Reported in the *New York Times,* 7 March, 1946.

13. Quoted in Halford E. Luccock, *Communicating the Gospel* (New York: Harper & Row, 1954) 133.

14. One of Reinhold Niebuhr's pithy phrases.

15. See Marshall Frady, *Billy Graham: A Parable of American Righteousness* (New York: Little, Brown, 1979) for a documented in-depth study of Billy Graham and his ministry in cultural context. For a perceptive critique of Frady's book (and Graham), see Barbara Grizzuti Harrison's review in *The New Republic,* vol. 181 (July 7 and 14, 1979), nos. 1 and 2, pp. 28-33. Her critique concludes: "Billy Graham—voted in 1970 one of the ten-best-dressed men in the world—says: 'I've never known a moment of despair.' The Gospel according to St. John says: 'Jesus wept,'" (p. 33). See also Elizabeth Hardwick, "The Portable Canterbury," *The New York Review of Books,* vol. 26, no. 13 (August 16, 1979), 3-6 for another insightful, thought-provoking review of Frady's book. Hardwick makes these two observations about the Nixon-Graham friendship: "Graham's polyethylene blandness met Nixon's polyethylene deceitfulness and these impervious surfaces were very agreeable." "And what did he (Graham) decide when he could no longer fail to name *something* askew in Nixon? 'I think it was sleeping pills. Sleeping pills and demons.'" p. 5. The reason for citing Frady's book here is that it reflects in

a focused way the anti-intellectual, individualistic, often self-righteous strain in American religious life. The sub-title, "A Parable of American Righteousness," is accurate. See also Richard Quebedeaux, *The Young Evangelicals* (New York: Harper & Row, 1974), and *The Worldly Evangelicals* (New York: Harper & Row, 1978), for accounts of the radical changes that are taking place in this wing of American Christianity.

16. See Martin E. Marty, *The Modern Schism* (New York: Harper & Row, 1969); also, Joseph Sittler, *The Ecology of Preaching: The New Situation in Preaching* (Philadelphia: Fortress, 1961), and Fernand Brandel, *Afterthoughts on Material Civilization and Capitalism*, trans., Patricia M. Ranum (Baltimore: Johns Hopkins University Press, 1977).

17. See Wallace E. Fisher, *Stand Fast in Faith* (New York: Abingdon, 1978), Chapter 1, on the need to get freedom and discipline into personal and social equilibrium. See also John W. Gardner, *Morale* (New York: Norton, 1978).

18. See, for example, Leon V. Sigal, "Rethinking the Unthinkable," *Foreign Policy*, No. 34, Spring 1979, 35-51.

19. See Richard Hofstadter, *The Paranoid Style in American Politics* (New York: Vintage, 1967), and *Anti-Intellectualism in American Life* (New York: Knopf, 1963); also Erling Jorstad, *The Politics of Doomsday: Fundamentalists of the Far Right* (New York: Abingdon, 1970).

20. Thor Hall, *The Future Shape of Preaching* (Philadelphia: Fortress, 1971) 70.

21. Donald McLeod, "Talk About Preaching," *The Christian Century*, Vol. XCV, No. 4, February 1-8, 1978, 98-102.

22. Colin Morris, *The Word and the Words* (New York: Abingdon, 1975) 26.

2. PREACHING IN TODAY'S THEOLOGICAL CONTEXT

1. This is one of the trenchant observations Arthur Koestler made about human nature during the rise of the Nazi state.

2. Henry Steele Commager, *The American Mind* (New Haven: Yale University Press, 1950) 410.

3. Edmund S. Morgan, *The Challenge of the American Revolution* (New York: Norton, 1976) 93.

4. For historical perspective, see John Kenneth Galbraith, *The Affluent Society*, 3rd, ed., rev. (New York: Houghton Mifflin, 1976), and Richard Klinger, *Simple Justice* (New York: Knopf, 1976).

5. I am indebted to W. E. Sangster for this phrasing.
6. See R. E. C. Browne, *The Ministry of the Word* (Philadelphia: Fortress, 1976) 86ff. First published, SCM, 1959.
7. Ibid., 16.
8. Ibid.
9. Quoted by Thomas Franklin O'Meara, "Is There a Common Authority for Christians?," *The Ecumenical Review*, XXII, January, 1970, 26.
10. Quoted in an unpublished lecture, "Word of God, Sacraments, and Ministry" by Theodore G. Tappert, late professor of church history, The Lutheran Theological Seminary at Philadelphia.
11. How one congregation tackled that—and still does—is described in detail in Fisher, *From Tradition to Mission*, chapters 3 through 5.
12. See Richard R. Niebuhr, *Resurrection and Historical Reason* (New York: Scribner, 1957); Wolfhart Pannenberg, *Essays on Old Testament Hermeneutics*, ed. by Claus Westermann, tr. by James Luther Mays (Richmond: John Knox, 1964); Rudolf Bultmann, *Existence and Faith*, ed., by Schubert Ogden (New York: Meridian, 1960), especially "Is Exegesis Without Presuppositions Possible?"; Paul Althaus, *Fact and Faith in the Kerygma of Today* (Philadelphia: Fortress, 1959); James Robinson, *A New Quest of the Historical Jesus* (London: SCM, 1959); Heinrich Ott, *The Historical Jesus and the Kerygmatic Christ*, tr. and ed. by Carl E. Braaten and Roy A. Harrisville (Nashville: Abingdon, 1964); Gunther Bornkamm, *Kerygma and History*, trans., and ed., by Carl E. Braaten and Roy A. Harrisville (Nashville: Abingdon, 1962). See also the Cambridge Press paperback (1978), *Christ, Faith and History*, which first appeared in hardback in 1972. Peter Carnley's essay, "The Poverty of Historical Criticism," is especially enlightening.
13. Alan Richardson, *History, Sacred and Profane* (Philadelphia: Westminster, 1964) 46-47.
14. Browne, *The Ministry of the Word*, 29.
15. See Gunther Bornkamm, *Jesus of Nazareth* (New York: Harper & Row, 1975), first English trans., 1959, and Wolfhart Pannenberg, *Jesus, God, and Man* (Philadelphia: Fortress, 1974). Norman Perrin judges Bornkamm's work to be "easily the best 'Jesus book' of our time." Perrin, *Rediscovering the Teaching of Jesus* (New York: Harper & Row, 1976) 250.
16. See C. S. Lewis, *The Space Triology* (New York: Macmillan, 1965), for a committed Christian's view of the Christ event in a life-packed universe.

17. Emil Brunner, *Truth as Encounter,* new ed. (Philadelphia: Westminster, 1964) 21.
18. Rice, *Interpretation and Imagination,* 15.
19. C. H. Dodd, *The Founder of Christianity* (London: Macmillan, 1970) 16.
20. James M. Rees, *Preaching God's Burning Word* (Collegeville, Minnesota: Liturgical Press, 1975) 9.

3. THE PREACHER'S CALL AND OFFICE

1. Gardner C. Taylor, *How Shall They Preach?* (Elgin, Illinois: Progressive Baptist Publishing House, 1977) 24.
2. Hendrik Kraemer, *A Theology of the Laity* (Philadelphia: Westminster, 1958) 95. For another point of view, see Ralph D. Bucy, *The New Laity* (Waco, Texas: Word, 1978).
3. H. Richard Niebuhr, *The Purpose of the Church and Its Ministry,* 79-83.
4. See Joseph Fichter, *Religion as an Occupation: A Study in the Sociology of Professions* (Notre Dame, Indiana: University of Notre Dame Press, 1961) for an in-depth study.
5. See Urban T. Holmes, III, *The Future Shape of Ministry* (New York: Seabury, 1971).
6. J. W. Stevenson, *God in My Unbelief* (New York: Harper & Row, 1963) 57.
7. See Søren Kierkegaard, *The Sickness Unto Death,* trans., by Walter Lowrie (Princeton: Princeton University Press, 1941).
8. Hall, *The Future Shape of Preaching,* 103.
9. Eduard Thurneysen, *A Theology of Pastoral Care* (Richmond: John Knox, 1962) 235.
10. See Seward Hiltner, *Theological Dynamics* (Nashville: Abingdon, 1972) 95ff.
11. Paul Jonas, "Home Thoughts from Abroad," *Harper's* April, 1977, 21. See also, Alexander Solzhenitsyn, "The Exhausted West," *Harvard Magazine,* July/August, 1978, 21-26; and reactions to it in *Time* 26 June 1978, 18, 21-22.
12. See Sloan Wilson, *What Shall We Wear to This Party?* (New York: Simon & Schuster, 1976), for a contemporary novelist's devastating critique of our "success-pleasure" culture; also Joseph Heller, *Something Happened* (New York: Knopf, 1974). T. S. Eliot, with the poet's heightened perception of reality, made this the theme of his celebrated work, *A Cocktail Party,* a half century ago.
13. Josephine Hendin, *Vulnerable People: A View of American Fiction Since 1945* (New York: Oxford University Press,

1978). See also Henry Nash Smith, *Democracy and the Novel: Popular Resistance to Classic American Writers* (New York: Oxford University Press, 1978), for public response to serious nineteenth-century novelists.

14. Jonas, "Home Thoughts from Abroad," *Harper's*, April, 1977, 23.

15. See Gabriel Fackre, *The Christian Story: A Narrative Presentation of Basic Christian Doctrine* (Grand Rapids: Eerdmans, 1978); also Robert Jenson, *Story and Promise* (Philadelphia: Fortress, 1973).

4. THE PREACHER'S—AND THE CONGREGATION'S— NEED TO GROW

1. Browne, *The Ministry of the Word*, 15.

2. Henry Ward Beecher, *Yale Lectures on Preaching*, First Series (New York: Ford, 1972) 61.

3. James S. Stewart, *Heralds of God* (London: Hodder & Stoughton, 1946) 104.

4. On changing perceptions of God, see Letty M. Russell, *Human Liberation in a Feminist Perspective: A Theology* (Philadelphia: Westminster, 1977); Rosemary R. Reuther, *Liberation Theology* (New York: Paulist, 1973); Rubem Alves, *A Theology of Human Hope* (New York: Corpus, 1969); Frederick Herzog, *Liberation Theology* (New York: Seabury, 1972); James Cone, *A Black Theology of Liberation* (New York: Lippincott, 1970).

5. Rees, *Preaching God's Burning Word*, 10.

6. Morris, *The Word and the Words*, 27.

7. Paul Scherer, *For We Have This Treasure* (New York: Harper & Row, 1944) 125.

8. Jürgen Moltmann, *The Church in the Power of the Spirit*, trans., Margaret Kohl (New York: Harper & Row, 1977) 103.

9. Farmer, *The Servant of the Word*, 2.

10. Quoted in Harry F. Baughman, *Jeremiah Today* (Philadelphia: Fortress, 1947) 37.

11. See Wallace E. Fisher, *Politics, Poker, and Piety: A Cultural Perspective on Religion in America* (Nashville: Abingdon, 1972), chapters 4, 5, and 6. See also, Robert Bellah, "Civil Religion in America," *Daedalus*, Winter, 1967. For a critique of Bellah's thesis, see John F. Wilson, "The Status of Civil Religion," Elwyn A. Smith, ed., *The Religion of the Republic* (Philadelphia: Fortress, 1971) 1-21.

12. Browne, *The Ministry of the Word,* 25. The parentheses are mine.
13. Roy Pearson, *The Ministry of Preaching* (New York: Harper & Row, 1959) 86.

5. ON PREPARING TO PREPARE THE SERMON
PART I

1. John V. Taylor, *The Go-Between God,* 3.
2. Olga Ivins Kaya, *A Captive of Time: My Years with Pasternak* (Garden City, New York: Doubleday, 1978) 138.
3. Dorothy Lobrano Guth, ed., *Letters of E. B. White* (New York: Harper & Row, 1976) 32.
4. Sittler, *The Ecology of Faith,* 4-5.
5. Gardner Taylor, *How Shall They Preach?,* 60.
6. Kevin Phillips, "The Balkanization of America," *Harper's,* May, 1978, vol. 256, no. 1536, 37-47. See also Michael Novak, *The Guns of Latimer* (New York: Basic Books, 1978).
7. Herbert Paul, ed., *Letters of Lord Acton to Mary, Daughter of the Right Honorable W. E. Gladstone* (London: George Allen, 1904) 6.
8. Ward and Dubos, *Only One Earth,* 11.
9. Roderick Nordell, "Take Jefferson's Advice—Read a Novel," *The Christian Science Monitor,* 19 June, 1977, 27.
10. Hendin, *Vulnerable People,* 212.
11. Gilbert Highet, *The Immortal Profession* (New York: Weybright & Talley, 1976) 4-5.
12. John H. Snow, *The Gospel in a Broken World* (Philadelphia: Westminster, 1974) 73.
13. William Temple, *Nature, Man, and God* (New York: Macmillan, 1939), and Reinhold Niebuhr, *The Nature and Destiny of Man* (New York: Macmillan, 1942).
14. Ernest Fremont Tittle, *The Foolishness of Preaching* (New York: Holt 1930) 304-305.
15. Somerset Maugham, *The Summing Up* (Garden City, New York: Doubleday, 1938) 87.

6. ON PREPARING TO PREPARE THE SERMON
PART II

1. Stewart, *Heralds of God,* Chapter 3, "The Preacher's Study."
2. See Sittler, *The Ecology of Faith,* Chapter 5, "Maceration of the Minister."
3. Browne, *The Ministry of the Word,* 86.

4. William Lawrence, *The Life of Phillips Brooks* (New York: Harper Row, 1930) 48.
5. Stevenson, *God in My Unbelief*, 7.
6. Fenelon, *Dialogues of Eloquence*, trans., Wilbur Samuel Howell (Princeton, New Jersey: Princeton University Press, 1951) 87.
7. To enrich our biblical preaching, we preachers need to study Joachim Jeremias, *The Parables of Jesus* (New York: Harper & Row, 1968); Sallie M. TeSelle, *Speaking in Parables: A Study in Metaphor and Theology* (Philadelphia: Fortress, 1975); Dan Otto Via, Jr., *The Parables: Their Literary and Existential Dimensions* (Philadelphia: Fortress, 1967); C. H. Dodd, *The Parables of the Kingdom* (New York: Scribner, 1961); Heinz Politzer, *Franz Kafka: Parable and Paradox* (Ithaca: Cornell University Press, 1962).
8. Stewart, *Heralds of God*, 105.
9. Highet, *The Immortal Profession*, 18.
10. C. S. Lewis, *Surprised by Joy*, first American edition (New York: Harcourt, Brace, 1956) 199-200.

7. THE BIBLICAL SERMON: WHAT IS IT?

1. See William Strunk, Jr., and E. B. White, *The Elements of Style*, second edition (New York and London: Macmillan, 1972), Chapter 5, "An Approach to Style."
2. Ferris, *Go Tell the People*, 17.
3. Peter Taylor Forsyth, *Positive Preaching and the Modern Mind* (London: Hodder & Stoughton, 1907) 3.
4. On teaching, see Gilbert Highet, *The Art of Teaching* (New York: Macmillan, 1951); Jacques Barzun, *The House of Intellect* (New York: Harper & Row, 1962); and Loren Eisley, *The Unexpected Universe* (New York: Macmillan, 1969).
5. Fisher, *Stand Fast in Faith*, chapters 2-5.
6. C. H. Dodd, *Apostolic Preaching and Its Development* (London: Macmillan, 1936).
7. James D. Smart, *The Teaching Ministry of the Church* (Philadelphia: Westminster, 1954) 11.
8. Søren Kierkegaard first made this penetrating observation.
9. Browne, *The Ministry of the Word*, 74. See also Smart, *The Teaching Ministry of the Church*, especially Chapters 1 and 7.
10. See Urban T. Holmes, *Ministry and Imagination* (New York: Seabury, 1976).
11. Halford Luccock, *In the Minister's Workshop* (New York: Harper & Row, 1943) 36.

12. See John Baillie, *The Sense of the Presence of God* (New York: Scribner, 1962).

13. Ferdinand Hahn, *The Worship of the Early Church* (Philadelphia: Fortress, 1974) 108. See also 2-3, 30-31, 38, 104-105. See also Gustaf Aulen, *The Drama and the Symbols*, trans., Sydney Linton (Philadelphia: Fortress, 1970), and Fisher, *From Tradition to Mission*, 129-132.

14. See Andre Parrot, *Golgotha and the Church of the Holy Sepulcher* (London: SCM, 1957) 45-46.

15. Peter Berger, *The Noise of Solemn Assemblies* (Garden City: Doubleday, 1961) 37.

16. Ferris, *Go Tell the People*, 31.

8. THE SERMON: ITS STRUCTURE

1. C. S. Lewis in his preface to Milton's *Paradise Lost*.

2. D. Martyn Lloyd-Jones, *Preaching and Preachers* (London: Hodder & Stoughton, 1971) 118-119.

3. Ferris, *Go Tell the People*, 7. The parentheses are mine.

4. Ibid., 82.

5. See A. J. Gossip, *The Hero in Thy Soul* (New York: Scribner, 1930) 106-116, for the sermon.

6. See Andrew Watterson Blackwood, *The Protestant Pulpit: An Anthology of Master Sermons from the Reformation to Our Own Day* (New York: Abingdon, 1957), 50-62 for Chalmers' sermon.

7. For fuller discussions on structuring sermons see, H. Grady Davis, *Design for Preaching* (Philadelphia: Fortress, 1956); W. E. Sangster, *The Craft of Sermon Construction* (Grand Rapids: Baker, 1972, reprint); and George E. Sweazey, *Preaching the Good News* (Englewood Cliffs, New Jersey: Prentice-Hall, 1976).

8. A. J. Gossip, *Experience Worketh Hope* (New York: Scribner, 1945) 102.

9. See Ferris, *Go Tell the People*, Chapter 4. The parenthetical descriptions are partially mine.

10. Martin Luther King, Jr., *Strength to Love*, memorial edition (New York: Pocket Books, 1968) 124-132.

9. THE INTRODUCTION AND CONCLUSION OF THE SERMON

1. Scherer, *For We Have This Treasure*, 143.

2. *The Preaching of Chrysostom: Homilies on the Sermon on the*

Mount, Introduction, Jaroslav Pelikan (Philadelphia: Fortress, 1967). Pelikan's critical essay on Chrysostom is instructive for preachers.

3. Walter J. Burghardt, "The Word Made Flesh Today," *New Catholic World,* vol. 221, no. 1323, May/June, 1978, 117.

4. Elton Trueblood, *The Yoke of Christ and Other Sermons* (New York: Harper & Row, 1958) 11-21.

5. Harry Emerson Fosdick, *On Being Fit to Live With: Sermons on Post-War Christianity* (New York: Harper & Row, 1946) 53.

6. John H. Jowett, *Great Pulpit Masters* (Grand Rapids, Michigan: Baker, 1972) 79.

7. Merrill R. Abbey, *Communication in Pulpit and Parish* (Philadelphia: Westminster, 1973) 176-178.

8. Quoted in Helmut Thielicke, *Encounter with Spurgeon* (New York: Harper & Row, 1966) 127.

9. See John Bartlow Martin, *Adlai Stevenson of Illinois: The Life of Adlai Stevenson* (Garden City, New York: Doubleday, 1976) for a detailed study of Stevenson's labors to make his speeches rational in thrust and polished in style.

10. Ferris, *Go Tell the People,* 69.

11. Sweazey, *Preaching the Good News,* 100-102.

12. Stewart, *Heralds of God,* 93.

13. Ferris, *Go Tell the People,* 97.

14. Black, *The Mystery of Preaching,* 103.

15. Ibid., 102-103.

16. See Frederick Zinsser, *On Writing Well* (New York: Harper & Row, 1976), Chapter 10, "The Ending," for solid guidance on writing conclusions.

17. Rice, *Interpretation and Imagination,* 109.

10. THE WORD OF GOD AND THE PREACHER'S WORDS

1. See Sissela Bok, *Lying: Moral Choice in Public and Private Life* (New York: Pantheon, 1978). A solid book for preachers in any era.

2. Zinsser, *On Writing Well,* 35.

3. See Winthrop S. Hudson, *The Great Tradition of the American Churches* (New York: Harper & Row, 1953). (Two chapters on the social impact of preaching.) Secular historians, J. R. Greene for example, credit Wesley and his lay preachers for improving the social character of England in the eighteenth century.

4. Strunk and White, *The Elements of Style,* 39-40.

5. Browne, *The Ministry of the Word*, 17.
6. In addition to E. B. White and Frederick Zinsser, these books will help the preacher to choose and use words more effectively: Rudolph Flesch, *A New Guide to Better Writing* (New York Popular Library, 1963); Jacques Barzun, *Simple and Direct* (New York: Harper & Row, 1975); Edwin Newman, *Strictly Speaking* (New York: Random House, 1975); Theodore M. Bernstein, *The Careful Writer: A Modern Guide to English Usage* (New York: Atheneum, 1977); Roget's Thesaurus, fourth ed.; and a good unabridged dictionary.
7. Browne, *The Ministry of the Word*, 30.
8. Another of Kierkegaard's penetrating phrases.
9. F. F. Bruce, *Paul: Apostle of the Heart Set Free* (Grand Rapids, Michigan: Eerdmans, 1978) 135f, and 456.
10. Leslie J. Tizard, *Preaching: The Art of Communication* (New York: Oxford University Press, 1959) 48.
11. Scherer, *For We Have This Treasure*, 204.
12. Ibid., 186.
13. See Fisher, *From Tradition to Mission*, chapters 3, 4, and 5, for a first-hand report on dialog in a particular congregation and community.
14. Walter J. Ong, *The Presence of the Word* (New Haven: Yale University Press, 1967) 1.
15. Quoted in Browne, *The Ministry of the Word*, 68.
16. *Luther's Works*, American edition, vol. 51, edited and translated by John W. Doberstein; General editor, Helmut Lehmann (Philadelphia: Fortress, 1959) 284-285.

NOW, FINALLY

1. Frederick Beuchner, *Telling the Truth: The Gospel as Tragedy, Comedy, and Fairy Tale* (New York: Harper & Row, 1977) 97.
2. G. K. Chesterton, quoted by James S. Stewart, *River of Life* (New York: Scribner 1962) 128.

Bibliography

ON PREACHING

Merrill R. Abbey, *Communication in Pulpit and Parish* (Philadelphia: Westminster, 1973). A practical, sane application of current communication theory to preaching. Stimulating.

Frederick W. Beuchner, *Telling the Truth: The Gospel as Tragedy, Comedy, and Fairy Tale* (New York: Harper & Row, 1977). A poet-preacher and a serious novelist who commands words to say precisely what he wants them to say.

———, *The Hungering Dark* (New York: Seabury, 1974). For his understanding of contemporary man and his proclamation of the gospel in haunting images.

Yngve Brilioth, *A Brief History of Preaching* (Philadelphia: Fortress, 1965). Limited to Continental preaching, it provides the preacher with perspective on preaching and culture.

Phillips Brooks, *Lectures on Preaching* (New York: Macmillan & Son, 1897). For his simple, luminous faith.

R. E. C. Browne, *The Ministry of the Word* (Philadelphia: Fortress, 1976). A theological study that can be reread profitably every three to five years.

Herbert H. Farmer, *The Servant of the Word* (Philadelphia: Fortress, 1964). Originally, Scribner's, 1942. Still the best book on the theology of preaching.

Theodore Parker Ferris, *Go Tell the People* (New York: Seabury, 1951). Simplicity, clarity, directness, practicality, and grace.

Peter Taylor Forsyth, *Positive Preaching and the Modern Mind* (London: Hodder & Stoughton, 1907). This prescient preacher, writing more than seven decades ago, is still pretty much on target.

Thor Hall, *The Future Shape of Preaching* (Philadelphia: Fortress, 1971). Presents a tenacious argument that the Word of God unifies the functions of ministry.

Reuel Howe, *Partners in Preaching* (New York: Seabury, 1967). Emphasizes the congregation's part in preaching.

Winthrop S. Hudson, *The Great Tradition of the American Churches* (New York: Harper & Row, 1953). Two excellent chapters on the influence of preaching on society.

Edgar DeWitt Jones, *The Royalty of the Pulpit* (New York: Harper & Row, 1951). A survey of the Beecher Lecturers. Perspective.

Henry Mitchell, *Black Preaching* (New York: Harper & Row, 1976). Sharp insights into the psychology of preaching to modern man, white as well as black.

H. Richard Niebuhr and Daniel D. Williams, *The Ministry in Historical Perspective* (New York: Harper & Row, 1956). Points up different kinds of communication between pulpit and pew over the centuries. Perspective.

Daniel T. Niles, *The Preacher's Calling to Be Servant* (London: Lutterworth, 1959). Urgent sense of "call" and biblical view of ministry.

Walter J. Ong, *The Presence of the Word* (New Haven: Yale University Press, 1967). A creative study: brilliant, indispensable.

Norman Perrin, *Rediscovering the Teaching of Jesus* (New York: Harper & Row, 1976). A solid challenge to those who still separate "historical knowledge of Jesus from Christological affirmation."

James H. Rees, *Preaching God's Burning Word* (Collegeville, Minnesota: The Liturgical Press, 1975). A clear-headed grasp of the difficulties of preaching in our culture.

Charles I. Rice, *Interpretation and Imagination* (Philadelphia: Fortress, 1970). Because he sends the preacher to novels, plays, and poetry for a fresh way of seeing reality *in the light of the gospel.*

Paul E. Scherer, *For We Have This Treasure* (New York: Harper & Row, 1945), and *The Word God Sent* (New York: Harper & Row, 1965). For his biblical theology, cultural perception, masterful use of the English language, and passionate sense of vocation.

Joseph Sittler, *The Anguish of Preaching* (Philadelphia: Fortress, 1961). Insightful, honest wrestling with the difficulties inherent in biblical preaching in our culture.

James S. Stewart, *Heralds of God* (Baker, 1972). One of the best volumes on the work of preaching in print.

Charles Smyth, *The Art of Preaching* (New York: Macmillan, 1940). A survey of preaching in the Church of England, 747-1939. Stresses the significance of language. Perspective.

Helmut Thielicke, *Encounter with Spurgeon* (Philadelphia: Fortress, 1963). Thielicke separates the wheat from the chaff in Spurgeon. His "encounter" will enrich the preacher.

Ernest Fremont Tittle, *The Foolishness of Preaching* (New York: Holt, 1930). Because I admire this man's courage for preaching boldly and perceptively to social issues—and paying the cost of it—when few other American parish preachers did either, 1920-1950.

Amos N. Wilder, *The Language of the Gospel: Early Christian Rhetoric* (New York: Harper & Row, 1964). An indispensable aid and challenge to preachers.

HELPFUL MANUALS ON PREACHING

Richard R. Caemmerer, *Preaching for the Church* (St. Louis: Concordia, 1959). Relentless focus on the kerygma and sane counsel to preachers.

H. Grady Davis, *Design for Preaching* (Philadelphia: Fortress, 1958). The best *manual* on preaching in print.

Halford E. Luccock, *In the Minister's Workshop* (New York: Harper & Row, 1943). A practical workbook with sparkle.

William E. Sangster, *The Craft of Sermon Construction* (Flint, Michigan: Baker, 1972). Shallow on content; deep on common sense. His types of sermons are abstruse to me.

George E. Sweazey, *Preaching the Good News* (Englewood, New Jersey: Prentice Hall, 1976). A no-nonsense manual on preaching. Comprehensive. Especially useful for seminarians and young preachers.

A SAMPLING OF PUBLISHED SERMONS

Karl Barth, *Deliverance of the Captives* (New York: Harper & Row, 1961).

Frederick W. Beuchner, *The Magnificent Defeat* (New York: Seabury, 1968).

Andrew W. Blackwood, *The Protestant Pulpit: An Anthology of Master Sermons from the Reformation to Our Own Day* (New York: Abingdon, 1957).

James W. Cox, ed., *The Twentieth Century Pulpit* (Nashville: Abingdon, 1978).

Joseph G. Donders, *Jesus, the Stranger: Reflections on the Gospels* (Maryknoll: Orbis, 1978).

Clyde E. Fant and William M. Pinson, Jr., eds., *Twenty Centuries of Great Preaching* (Waco: Wood, 1971).

Theodore Parker Ferris, *When I Became a Man* (New York: Macmillan, 1953).

Harry Emerson Fosdick, *On Being Fit to Live With* (New York: Harper & Row, 1946).

Arthur John Gossip, *From the Edge of the Crowd* (Edinburgh: T & T Clark, 1924); *The Galilean Accent* (Edinburgh: T & T Clark, 1927); *The Hero in Thy Soul* (New York: Scribner, 1930); *Experience Worketh Hope* (New York: Scribner, 1945); and *In the Secret Place of the Most High* (New York: Scribner, 1946).

Martin Luther King, Jr., *Strength to Love* (New York: Pocket Books, 1968). The best example of prophetic-pastoral preaching in America, 1950-1968.

Reinhold Niebuhr, *Justice and Mercy* (New York: Harper & Row, 1974).

David Roberts, *The Grandeur and Misery of Man* (New York: Harper & Row, 1955).

Frederick W. Robertson, *The Preaching of F. W. Robertson* (Philadelphia: Fortress, 1964).

James S. Stewart, *A Faith to Proclaim* (New York: Scribner, 1958).

Paul Tillich, *The Shaking of the Foundations* (New York: Harper & Row, 1951).

THE PARISH

Tom Allan, *The Face of My Parish* (London: Macmillan, 1954). Person-centered evangelical fervor and cultural realism.

Georges Bernanos, *The Diary of a Country Priest* (New York: Harper & Row, 1953). A classic. Every ordained minister should read it—twice, or more.

Wallace E. Fisher, *From Tradition to Mission* (Nashville: Abingdon, 1965). For an unvarnished first-hand account of what happens when the concepts in this book on preaching are actualized in a particular congregation.

Conrad Richter, *A Simple, Honorable Man* (New York: Knopf, 1962). A winsome story of God's grace in action. This novel, more than any other I know, presents a biblical view of ministry.

J. W. Stevenson, *God in My Unbelief* (New York: Harper & Row, 1963). A compassionate view of the parish which does not prostitute God's Word.

CHURCH AND SOCIETY

Sydney E. Ahlstrom, *Religious History of the American People* (New Haven: Yale University Press, 1972).

Karl Barth, *Community, State, and Church* (New York: Doubleday, 1960).

C. E. Black, *The Dynamics of Modernization* (New York: Harper, 1967).

Christopher Freedman and Marie Jahoda, *World Futures: The Great Debate* (New York: Universe, 1978). Indispensable.

Josephine Hendin, *Vulnerable People* (New York: Oxford University Press, 1978).

Kenneth Galbraith, *The Affluent Society* (New York: Random House, 1959). Fundamentally important.

Langdon Gilkey, *How Can the Church Minister to the World without Losing Itself?* (New York: Harper & Row, 1964).

James M. Gustafson, *Can Ethics Be Christian?* (Chicago: University of Chicago Press, 1977).

Richard M. Heiber, *The American Idea of Success* (New York: McGraw-Hill, 1971).

Geoffrey Hodgson, *America in Our Time* (Garden City, New York: Doubleday, 1976).

Christopher Lasch, *The Culture of Narcissism: American Life in an Age of Diminishing Expectations* (New York: Norton, 1978). Fundamentally important.

Robert H. Lifton, *Boundaries: Psychological Man in Revolution* (New York: Vantage, 1970).

Richard John Neuhaus, *Christian Faith and Public Policy* (Minneapolis: Augsburg, 1977).

H. Richard Niebuhr, *Christ and Culture* (New York: Harper & Row, 1956). A classic. Indispensable.

Henry Nash Smith, *Democracy and the Novel* (New York: Oxford University Press, 1978).

Ronald H. Stone, *Reinhold Niebuhr: Prophet to Politicians* (Nashville: Abingdon, 1972).

Tad Szulc, *The Illusion of Peace: Foreign Policy in the Nixon Years* (New York: Viking, 1978).

David Vogel, *Lobbying the Corporation: Citizen Challenges to Business Authority* (New York: Basic Books, 1979).

Barbara Ward and Renee Dubos, *Only One Earth: The Care and Maintenance of a Small Planet* (New York: Norton, 1972). Indispensable.

Robert Penn Warren, *Democracy and Poetry* (Cambridge: Harvard University Press, 1975).

John Howard Yoder, *The Politics of Jesus* (Grand Rapids: Eerdmans, 1972). Indispensable.

THE PASTOR'S LIBRARY

The Bible—in various translations for those who, like me, cannot read Hebrew or Greek (KJV, RSV, NEB, GNB, Moffatt, Knox, Smith and Goodspeed, Weymouth, Philips, Basic English, Cotton Patch Version).

See *Essential Books for a Pastor's Library* (Richmond: Union Theological Seminary, 1976). Annotated by Union's faculty. To my knowledge, the best guide in print. See also chapters 5 and 6 in this work and the Notes.

21
24
25
28
50
55
57
59
63